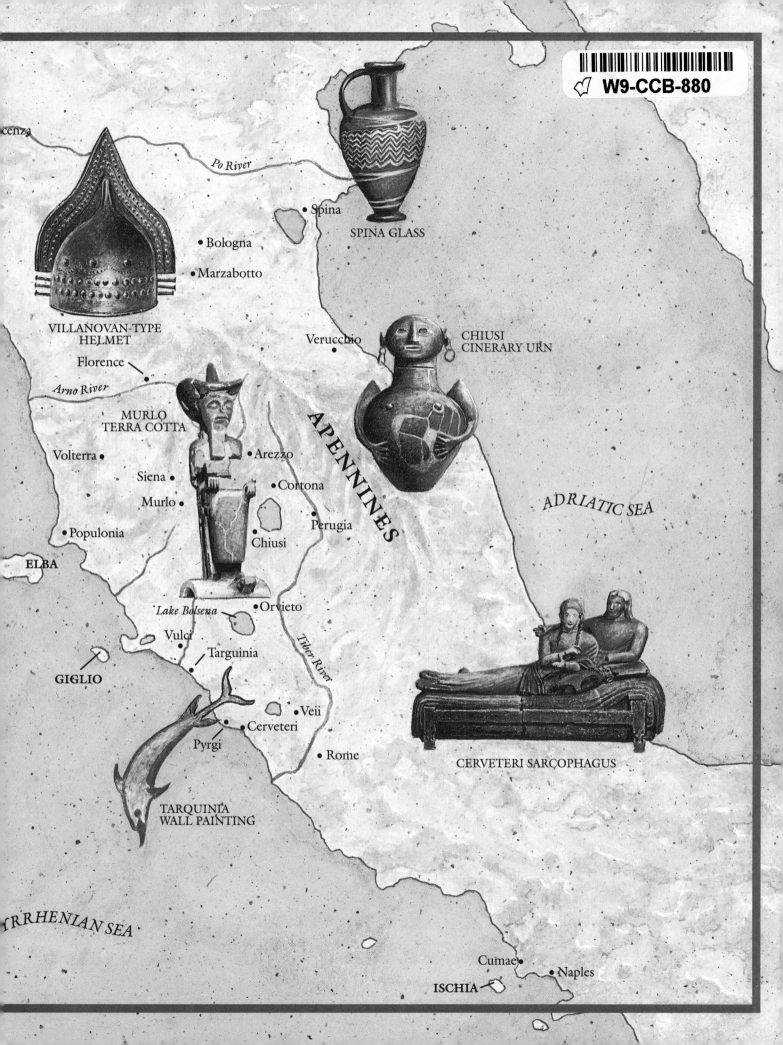

Po River

• Spina

SPINA GLASS

• Bologna

• Marzabotto

cenza

**VILLANOVAN-TYPE
HELMET**

Florence

Arno River

• Verucchio

**CHIUSI
CINERARY URN**

**MURLO
TERRA COTTA**

Volterra •

• Arezzo

A
P
E
N
N
I
N
E
S

Siena •

• Cortona

Murlo •

Perugia

ADRIATIC SEA

• Populonia

Chiusi

ELBA

Lake Bolsena

• Orvieto

Vulci •

Tiber River

• Targuinia

GIGLIO

• Veii

• Cerveteri

Pyrgi

• Rome

CERVETERI SARCOPHAGUS

**TARQUINIA
WALL PAINTING**

TRRHENIAN SEA

Cumae •

• Naples

ISCHIA

TIME® LIFE BOOKS

Other Publications:

THE TIME-LIFE COMPLETE
  GARDENER
THE NEW HOME REPAIR AND
  IMPROVEMENT
JOURNEY THROUGH THE MIND
  AND BODY
WEIGHT WATCHERS® SMART CHOICE
  RECIPE COLLECTION
TRUE CRIME
THE AMERICAN INDIANS
THE ART OF WOODWORKING
ECHOES OF GLORY
THE NEW FACE OF WAR
HOW THINGS WORK
WINGS OF WAR
CREATIVE EVERYDAY COOKING
COLLECTOR'S LIBRARY OF THE
  UNKNOWN
CLASSICS OF WORLD WAR II
TIME-LIFE LIBRARY OF CURIOUS AND
  UNUSUAL FACTS
AMERICAN COUNTRY
VOYAGE THROUGH THE UNIVERSE
THE THIRD REICH
THE TIME-LIFE GARDENER'S GUIDE
MYSTERIES OF THE UNKNOWN
TIME FRAME
FIX IT YOURSELF
FITNESS, HEALTH & NUTRITION
SUCCESSFUL PARENTING
HEALTHY HOME COOKING
UNDERSTANDING COMPUTERS
LIBRARY OF NATIONS
THE ENCHANTED WORLD
THE KODAK LIBRARY OF CREATIVE
  PHOTOGRAPHY
GREAT MEALS IN MINUTES
THE CIVIL WAR
PLANET EARTH
COLLECTOR'S LIBRARY OF THE CIVIL
  WAR
THE EPIC OF FLIGHT
THE GOOD COOK
WORLD WAR II
THE OLD WEST

*For information on and a full description of
any of the Time-Life Books series listed above,
please call 1-800-621-7026 or write:*
Reader Information
Time-Life Customer Service
P.O. Box C-32068
Richmond, Virginia 23261-2068

Cover: In its vibrancy, this graceful terra-cotta head suggests the lively culture that produced it. Found at a temple site at the Etruscan port town of Pyrgi, it may have capped a fourth-century-BC statue of a marine goddess. Behind the head is a limestone cremation urn in the shape of a second-century-BC Etruscan house.

End paper: The map shows the range of Etruscan sites in Italy, while the heartland of Etruria can be seen shaded in the inset. Representative artifacts appear near their discovery sites. The map was painted by the artist Paul Breeden on paper textured to represent frescoes found on tomb walls. Breeden also painted the images illustrating the timeline on pages 158-159.

ETRUSCANS:
ITALY'S LOVERS
OF LIFE

Ex Líbrís

Randy Manning

Time-Life Books is a division of TIME LIFE INC.

PRESIDENT and CEO: John M. Fahey Jr.

EDITOR-IN-CHIEF: John L. Papanek

TIME-LIFE BOOKS

MANAGING EDITOR: Roberta Conlan

Director of Design: Michael Hentges
Director of Editorial Operations: Ellen Robling
Director of Photography and Research: John Conrad Weiser
Senior Editors: Russell B. Adams Jr., Dale M. Brown, Janet Cave, Lee Hassig, Robert Somerville, Henry Woodhead
Special Projects Editor: Rita Thievon Mullin
Director of Technology: Eileen Bradley
Library: Louise D. Forstall

PRESIDENT: John D. Hall

Vice President, Director of Marketing: Nancy K. Jones
Vice President, Director of New Product Development: Neil Kagan
Vice President, Book Production: Marjann Caldwell
Production Manager: Marlene Zack
Quality Assurance Manager: James King

Library of Congress Cataloging in Publication Data
Etruscans: Italy's lovers of life / by the editors of Time-Life Books.
p.   cm.— (Lost civilizations)
Includes bibliographical references and index.
ISBN 0-8094-9045-5
1. Etruscans.
I. Time-Life Books. II. Series.
DG223.E764 1995
937'.5—dc20   94-43686
                                            CIP

LOST CIVILIZATIONS

SERIES EDITOR: Dale M. Brown
Administrative Editor: Philip Brandt George

Editorial staff for *Etruscans: Italy's Lovers of Life*
Art Director: Bill McKenney
Picture Editor: Paula York-Soderlund
Text Editors: Charles J. Hagner (principal), Russell B. Adams Jr., Charlotte Anker
Associate Editors/Research-Writing: Mary Grace Mayberry, Katherine L. Griffin, Narisara Murray, Jarelle S. Stein
Senior Copyeditor: Mary Elizabeth Oelkers-Keegan
Picture Coordinator: Catherine Parrott
Editorial Assistant: Patricia D. Whiteford

Special Contributors: Anthony Allan, Ellen Galford, Donál Kevin Gordon (text); Craig Allen, Ann-Louise G. Gates, Ylann Schemm (research); Roy Nanovic (index)

Correspondents: Elisabeth Kraemer-Singh (Bonn), Christine Hinze (London), Christina Lieberman (New York), Maria Vincenza Aloisi (Paris). Valuable assistance was also provided by: Angelika Lemmer (Bonn); Judy Aspinall (London); Elizabeth Brown (New York); Leonora Dodsworth, Ann Wise (Rome); Dick Berry (Tokyo)

The Consultants:
Archaeologist Larissa Bonfante, professor of Classics at New York University, is a member of the Istituto di Studi Etruschi e Italici and the German Archaeological Institute. Her books include *Etruscan Dress; Out of Etruria: Etruscan Influence North and South; Etruscan Life and Afterlife, a Handbook of Etruscan Studies;* and *Reading the Past: Etruscan.*

Nancy Thomson de Grummond, professor of classics at Florida State University, has directed excavations since 1983 at the Etruscan/Romans site of Cetamura del Chianti in Tuscany. Her specialties include Etruscan and Roman art and the history of archaeology, and she has published numerous books, including *A Guide to Etruscan Mirrors.*

Archaeologist Erik O. Nielsen is Vice President for Academic Affairs and Chairman of the Archaeology/Art History Department at the University of Evansville in Indiana. Since 1982 he has been the director of excavations at Poggio Civitate, near Murlo, Italy. He has studied, written, and lectured on Etruscan artifacts and culture, and is a member of the Istituto di Studi Etruschi e Italici.

Special Correspondent:
The staff is especially indebted to Ann Natanson, Time-Life Books' correspondent in Rome for 30 years. She contributed invaluable research for the text and for the illustrations in this volume on Etruria. The Etruscans are one of her favorite subjects in a career rich with varied interests.

This volume is one in a series that explores the worlds of the past, using the finds of archaeologists and other scientists to bring ancient peoples and their cultures vividly to life.

Other volumes in the series include:

ETRUSCANS: ITALY'S LOVERS OF LIFE

By the Editors of Time-Life Books

TIME-LIFE BOOKS, ALEXANDRIA, VIRGINIA

CONTENTS

In the moody light of evening, a rocky outcrop in the heart of Italy's Tuscany gives no hint of the glory that once rested on its crown. There, 2,500 years ago, sat Volterra, one of the noblest and largest cities of Etruria, ringed by walls four or five miles in circumference. Coming upon the ruins of the ramparts for the first time, a 19th-century English traveler described these "mere fragments" as still being "so vast, that fable and song may well report them 'Piled by the hands of giants, / For god-like kings of old.'"

DISCOVERING THE FIRST ITALIANS

An Italian artifact predating Rome's greatness by several hundred years, this bronze flask from the late eighth century BC originated during the Villanovan, or proto-Etruscan, period (1000 to 700 BC). The bronze-working skill heralds beauties of Etruscan art yet to come.

Even for Italy, where the ancient past seems to lie all about and museums are filled with treasures dug from the earth, it was a major find. And as so often happens in a land where archaeological sites abound, the discovery occurred accidentally. When workers widening the main road to Rimini on the Adriatic coast in 1968 sliced through a series of burials near the small town of Verucchio, exposing a number of urns and other artifacts, no one was terribly surprised. Still, the roadwork was called to a halt while the appropriate authorities were notified, and Gino Vinicio Gentili, then the archaeological superintendent of the Emilia-Romagna region, came to inspect. "I saw right away there was interesting material," he said, "a bronze vase in a kylix shape, carved wood, gold plaques, and amber." Rescue excavations commenced the following year, and by 1972 more than 150 burials had been uncovered.

Pulses quickened again in September and October of that year, when almost 10 feet down, the porous topsoil gave way to nonporous clay and Gentili and his assistants came upon two burial pits that had been sealed for centuries in an airless mix of water and mud. Protected by the slime from insects and decay-causing bacteria, a ceiling of stout oak timbers supported by a pair of crossbeams still covered the first chamber, and two tree trunks served as columns. Around the columns lay a helmet, a bronze situla, or urn, and a large

Italian excavator Sergio Sani lifts three dishes, still holding the residue of a funeral banquet, from a wooden table submerged in Verucchio's Tomb 85. Concerned a sudden cave-in might rebury the seventh-century-BC tomb, Sani spent nearly 48 hours nonstop in the water and mud to retrieve the artifacts during the 1972 digging season.

pot holding amber and gold pins and other items. Miraculously, the tomb also contained a treasure trove of usually perishable artifacts, including remnants of three round, three-legged tables, a throne, and a footstool, all carved of wood; a length of woven linen wrapped around a vase holding human ashes; and straw baskets.

So complete was the preservation that Gentili was even able to identify the remnants of a funeral banquet that had been laid out at the time of interment, more than 2,500 years before. In different bowls on one of the three tables were the remains of grapes and hazelnuts, while covered pots on another table contained evidence of hare and fish.

The second tomb, a wooden burial box measuring more than seven feet long and almost four feet wide, lay just a few yards from the first. Inside rested an extravagantly crested bronze helmet that had probably been worn on ceremonial occasions, pieces of gold and amber, and more well-preserved wooden artifacts—a footstool, the handle of a now-vanished feathered fan, bowls with lids, and the handle of a metal ax—as well as woven wool and linen cloth, some of the pieces bearing a plaid pattern.

Gentili discovered the most impressive artifact by far not inside the burial box, but in a sodden mass on top of it: a collapsed second wooden throne, this one adorned with charming intaglios of men and women weaving, dyeing, parading, and riding in chariots. Ingeniously reconstructed later from its numerous fragments *(pages 12-13)*, the throne gave scholars new insight into daily life in Italy around 700 BC. More important, however, it and the other grave gifts presented compelling evidence that the people laid to rest around Verucchio were some of the earliest members of an intrigu-

Amber disks decorate a broken, but still beautiful, fibula found in Tomb 85 (above). Other items from the same site in-cluded materials rarely preserved in an-cient burials, among them the wicker in-terior of the helmet below. The wicker is laminated with small bronze studs, which form circular patterns around several bronze plates.

ing ancient culture centered between the Arno and Tiber Rivers on the Tyrrhenian side of the boot of Italy—that of the Etruscans.

Few civilizations have shone so brightly and faded as quickly. Bursting from a relatively small homeland, about the size of West Virginia or Wales, the Etruscans in the seventh century BC expand-ed west and south, to found colonies on the Tyrrhenian island of Corsica and near Naples and to create a cluster of settlements that gave them control over much of the fertile region known today as Campania. In the following century, they moved north, across the Apennines into the Po valley, setting up a chain of towns along the Adriatic coast. Most important for posterity, from the end of the sev-enth century BC until 510 BC they provided a dynasty that ruled Rome itself. In the words of the Roman historian Livy, Etruria at the height of its power "filled the whole length of Italy from the Alps to the Sicilian strait with the fame of her name."

But the Etruscans are re-membered for more than

A REGAL CHAIR REASSEMBLED FROM FRAGMENTS RECOVERED IN A TOMB

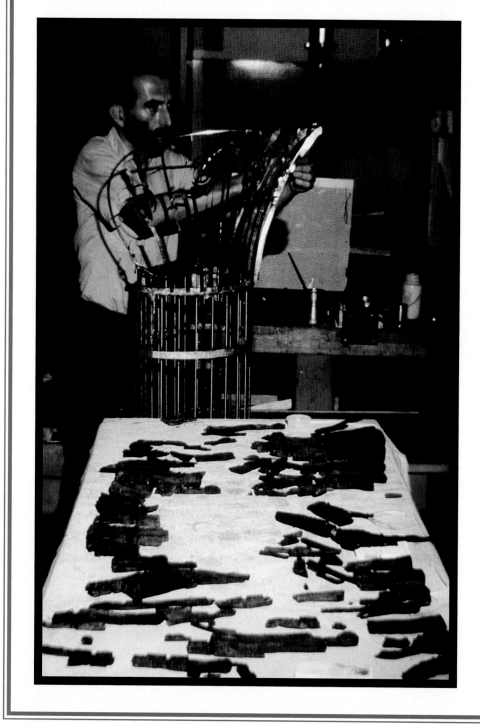

Of all the artifacts unearthed at the sprawling burial site discovered at Verucchio, Italy, in 1968, the most extraordinary was the wooden throne that had once graced the waterlogged crypt of an Etruscan noble. Not only was it a singular example of woodworking, but the decorative scenes depicted on the throne's flared arms and back gave archaeologists a unique glimpse of everyday life in the region during the seventh century BC. Even more astonishing, the piece had survived—wood rarely turns up intact at ancient sites.

When first found, however, the throne looked like little more than a mud-crusted clump of fragments. It would take three years of painstaking toil by the Italian restorer Giovanni Morigi—shown working at left—to return the throne to a semblance of its original appearance. Morigi's first task was to conserve the wood that had survived in the airless, watery environment of the tomb. This he achieved by treating the more than 250 fragments with polyethylene glycol, a synthetic wax that saturates ancient woods and prevents them from drying out and crumbling. Then he began putting these pieces back together, meticulously matching up the decorative scenes and patterns that were carved on both sides. As a guide to the general shape of the throne, Morigi referred to a relatively intact bronze throne and bits of a wooden one that archaeologists had unearthed in the same general area. Finally, Morigi fashioned a stainless steel framework upon which to affix the fragments. The upper section, representing the arms and back, was carefully braced with thin steel strips that allowed the attached pieces to be viewed from both sides.

The rear of the throne features elaborate geometric patterns. The front is carved with scenes presented in two distinct horizontal bands. On the lower band men in horse-drawn carts ride toward some unknown destination. In the band above them are detailed depictions of buildings; inside, two women, each with a waist-length braid, twist yarn on a spindle, while other women labor at upright looms in the background outside.

As detailed in the drawing below, this carving from the Verucchio throne portrays two women with a spindle. The two figures atop the house are decorative wooden monkeys, a common motif of the time.

Shown with all its preserved fragments assembled on a supporting steel frame, the Verucchio throne clearly displays its former splendor. By examining the matched grain of the wood, restorer Giovanni Morigi was able to determine that the throne had been carved from a single oak trunk measuring about a yard wide.

their temporal power alone. Counted among the most advanced civilizations of their time in the Western world, they were first-class engineers, renowned for road and bridge making as well as for ambitious irrigation works. Their potters, metalworkers, and goldsmiths were internationally recognized for their skills and for the innovative uses to which they put them. Modern dentists, for example, still admire the quality of the gold bridgework displayed in the mouths of cadavers from Etruscan tombs *(page 99)*.

They were also—again in Livy's words—"a people more than any other devoted to religious customs," showing a profound and fatalistic sense of the role divine forces play in shaping the course of human destiny. Yet their art jubilantly communicates an enjoyment of life's everyday pleasures, from banqueting to sports and games. Above all they appreciated music; according to classical commentators, the sounds of the pipe and lyre accompanied even the meanest of their daily activities.

They exerted long-lasting influence on later Western cultures, principally as a result of the sway they exercised over Rome in the century before the founding of the Republic. A surprising number of the symbols commonly regarded as Roman, from the ceremonial toga and Roman numerals to the bundle of rods known as the fasces—the emblem of Roman magistrates, revived in the 1920s by the Italian dictator Benito Mussolini as representative of Fascism—were in fact inherited from their neighbors and onetime rulers. It was the Etruscans too who passed on to the Romans their love of monumental art and architecture and an Italian version of the Greek gods, together with the technique of divination. Spurinna, the soothsayer who warned Julius Caesar to beware the ides of March in 44 BC, was of Etruscan origin. And most significant of all, the Etruscans bequeathed to Rome the secrets of writing and the alphabet.

Eventually, though, the precocious pupil overtook and overwhelmed its teacher, and Etruria was brought under the dominion of the Roman Empire. From the fourth century BC onward, its cities one by one accepted Roman overlordship, and by 89 BC, when Roman citizenship was conferred on all Etruscans, even their language had begun to fall into disuse. Yet long after imperial Rome itself crumbled and fell, treasure hunters, archaeologists, and scholars would set about the task of rediscovering the vivid, preclassical period that the Romans had eclipsed, and over the years they would astonish the world with their discoveries.

Clouds hover above the Etruscan island of Elba, one of the richest sources of iron in ancient times. The great smelting furnaces there inspired the Greeks to name the island Aethalia, from their word for smoke, "which lies," wrote the historian Diodorus Siculus, "so thick about it."

Ancient Etruria was made up of the present-day Italian province of Tuscany, along with parts of Latium to the south and Umbria to the east. The region divides naturally into two sections: a rolling plateau shaped by ancient volcanic activity and bordered to the south by a broad coastal plain known as the Maremma, and a rugged shoreline and a region of hill towns and wide alluvial valleys dominating the north.

The Etruscans were fortunate to inherit such land; their period of glory can be related directly to the exploitation of the resources it offered. The soil was exceptionally productive. According to the Greek historian Diodorus Siculus, it bore a wide variety of crops. The Etruscans, he wrote, "enjoy no lack of fruits, not only sufficient for their sustenance but contributing to abundant enjoyment and luxury." And though the broad plain that backs most of the region's coast is now almost harborless, in Etruscan times it was dotted with lagoons, long since silted up, that provided sheltered anchorages suitable for the needs of fishing and trading. Blessed with easy access to the sea, the Etruscans soon developed a reputation as skilled sailors—and feared pirates. According to a passage written in the fourth century BC by the Greek historian Ephorus, Etruscan freebooters were prowling the seas around Sicily as early as the eighth century BC.

The greatest of Etruria's natural resources, however, lay hidden beneath the soil. The mineral wealth of the Tolfa Hills near Civitavecchia in the south and of the Colline Metallifere—literally, the metal-bearing hills—near Siena in the north was matched only by that of the island of Elba, eight miles offshore. Through these reserves Etruria controlled the only considerable sources of copper, iron ore, and perhaps tin in the entire central Mediterranean region. The metals were exploited on a massive scale, and whole cities like Populonia, on the coast opposite Elba, grew up because of them. Indeed, archaeologists have found workings going back as far as the eighth century BC, complete with shafts, tunnels, subterranean galleries, cone-shaped smelters, and giant slag heaps. The piles were so extensive that they could be reprocessed during World War II to yield metal remaining in them for the Italian armaments industry.

The fame of the Etruscan mines spread rapidly across the Mediterranean world, and a trading network sprang up to handle their production. Greeks and Phoenicians brought luxury goods to swap for the precious ores, and the Etruscans grew wealthy on the exchange. The tide of riches ebbed and flowed between several dif-

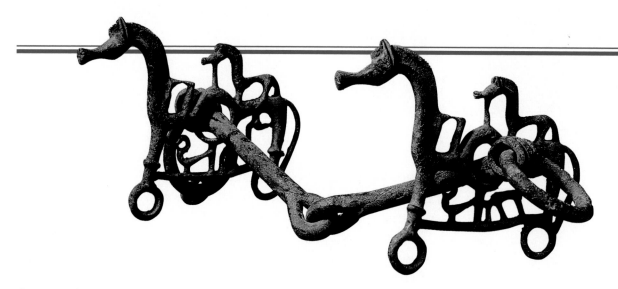

ferent urban centers over the centuries, for while an Etruscan civilization surely flowered—with its own language, religion, and customs—a unified Etruscan state never took shape.

Rather, Etruria in its heyday was divided between city-states much like those that made up contemporary Greece or Renaissance Italy some 2,000 years later. Classical writers spoke of 12 peoples of Etruria, and there seem to have been about a dozen such small sovereign territories, though over time some of these centers fell into decline and lost their place to newcomers. Unwilling or unable to make common cause, the cities jealously guarded their independence and competed economically. Literary sources hint that they even waged wars with each other.

According to Roman authors the Etruscans referred to themselves as Rasna or Rasenna. The Greeks, on the other hand, knew them as the Tyrrhenoi, thereby supplying the root of the word by which the waters between Italy and the islands of Corsica and Sardinia are known today—the Tyrrhenian Sea. To the Romans they were the Etrusci or Tusci, from which are derived the words Etruscan and Tuscany, respectively.

The fate of such names mirrors that of the civilization as a whole, for most of what is known about the Etruscans has come from other people. Though they almost certainly had a literature of their own, it is now lost. The folded linen on which

Two tiny horses ride the backs of a larger pair (above), *creating a stylized set of rein rings for this bronze horse bit from the second half of the eighth century BC. Horse bits, symbols of wealth and social status, began appearing in tombs during the late Villanovan period.*

An eighth-century-BC bronze worker incised this belt plaque (below) *with swirling abstract and geometric designs. Lozenge-shaped belt plaques such as this one were widely distributed in Italy and exported as far as Euboea, a Greek island in the western Aegean.*

their books were first written fell to dust long ago, and more important, the works ceased to be copied when the language died. The lack of texts makes it all but impossible to hear the Etruscans' own voices; instead, historians must make do with the accounts of their contemporaries, the Greeks and the Romans.

Given that these classical civilizations were longtime rivals of the Etruscans, it is hardly surprising that the picture they give of them is not entirely a flattering one. To be sure, some writers conceded good points: The fifth-century-BC Greek poet Pherecrates admitted the Etruscans were "skilled and loving craftsmen," an opinion seconded by his contemporary, the Athenian Critias. "Their bronzes of

Atop an eighth-century-BC, foot-high bronze vase (below), armed men circle a chained animal as a spearman (lower right) raises his weapon to slay a bullock in what appears to be a ritual dance. Villanovan artists created human figures that were stylized or rough in form, but expressed a spontaneous vitality.

every sort for the decoration and service of houses are best," he noted. But most historians held the Etruscans' love of beautiful objects as a mark of decadence. According to the first-century-BC historian Dionysius of Halicarnassus, they were "a people of dainty and expensive tastes, both at home and in the field carrying about with them, besides the necessities, costly and artistic articles of all kinds designed for pleasure and luxury."

The imputation of decadence, however, came across most strongly in prurient descriptions of the Etruscans' supposedly loose sexual morals. The many banquet scenes the Etruscans painted on the walls of their tombs certainly suggest that they enjoyed life to the full. But the views perpetuated by outsiders were probably based on a misunderstanding of the relationship of the sexes in Etruscan society. Men and women mixed together much more freely than in contemporary Greece, where only prostitutes dined in public with men. Seeing husbands and wives enjoying each other's company at banquets, hostile outsiders easily mistook the relative independence of the women for debauchery.

Such misconceptions would matter little if other sources existed to balance the picture. But in the centuries after Etruria was swallowed up by imperial Rome, cursory references made by the classical authors became the Etruscans' only epitaph. True, Claudius I, Roman emperor from AD 41 to 54, is said to have written a lengthy history of the Etruscans, but it too has been lost, leaving only the accounts of writers such as Livy to ensure that the Etruscans' role in Rome's early history was not forgotten entirely.

Yet as the classical world fell into decline and the Dark Ages spread across Europe, the memory of Etruria as a separate entity faded. By medieval times, what little was recalled became mixed with elements of fantasy and legend. A bizarre traveler's tale penned by the 12th-century English chronicler William of Malmesbury is typical. He described a monk who recounted seeing a "perforated" mountain in Italy in which the treasures of the Roman emperor Augustus

The scene above may look like a typical dig in progress, as two restorers uncover artifacts from an eighth-century-BC Etruscan burial, while a colleague records the positions in a drawing. But the setting is unusual. The earth in which the objects lie buried has been brought intact, in a massive block, to the laboratory, to enable the researchers to examine it under controlled conditions.

The method is complex and expensive. Site conditions must be suitable, and moving a find is grueling work. Fortunately for the team, led by Italian archaeologist Anna-Maria Esposito at the small necropolis of Casale Marittimo, financing was available. Moreover, the burial, known as Tomb G, lay just 20 inches down, in unrocky terrain. The archaeologists had first to scoop away the soil around and beneath the area, sliding planks under the burial itself to provide a platform, then build a box around the two tons of earth and artifacts that composed the freed block. Next, a crane lifted the crate onto a truck for the 30-mile journey to Florence.

Transporting a discovery from field to laboratory provides archaeologists with a rare gift—that of time. On site, work can be threatened by adverse conditions—weather and thieves, among other things—compelling the scientists to proceed faster than they might wish. In the lab, they can go as slowly and painstakingly as they like. Such meticulousness allowed Tomb G's researchers to re-create a unique ax handle (curved for throwing) from the position of the plaquettes that once decorated it.

Even some 19th-century archaeologists found the rewards of indoor excavation worth the pains. In the 1880s at Vetulonia, Italian Etruscologist Isidoro Falchi enclosed a large bronze cauldron, still filled with earth and burial goods, in plaster and wood and sent it over rough terrain to Florence. In contrast to his modern colleagues, however, Falchi excavated his find during a grand ceremony, attended by the prince of Naples himself.

were rumored to be hidden. "Many persons were reported to have entered into these caverns for the purpose of exploring them, and to have there perished," Malmesbury quotes the monk as saying. "We saw the way strewed with bare bones." Scholars assume that the picture of the perforated mountain may have been inspired by tombs such as those near Norchia that the Etruscans cut into the face of rocky cliffs. The description of the bones may also be based on actual Etruscan remains, only greatly exaggerated.

By the time of the Renaissance, an admiration for past civilizations replaced Malmesbury's feelings of awe, and curiosity about the Etruscans grew among such inquisitive and inventive souls as Annio of Viterbo, a Dominican friar. He took the first step toward reviving Etruscan studies by publishing inscriptions—some of which he had gathered near his hometown, in the heart of what had been Etruria, and others that he invented, no one knows why.

Slowly, a study of Etruscology developed. While holding the chair of civil law at the University of Pisa in the 17th century, Thomas Dempster, an eccentric Scottish scholar renowned in his day for his pugnacity as well as his wide learning, made a longer lasting contribution to the understanding of the Etruscans. Though it was said of him that "not a day passed that he did not use either his fists or his sword," Dempster was commissioned by the grand duke of Tuscany to write a history of the Etruscans. The resulting work, *De Etruria Regali Libri Septem* (Seven Books on Etruria of the Kings), gathered everything then written about the Etruscans into one encyclopedic tome, but for reasons that remain obscure it went unpublished for almost a hundred years.

Then an Englishman in Florence named Thomas Coke discovered Dempster's manuscript, added handsome copperplate illustrations and notes penned by a respected antiquarian, and in 1723 published it. The book appealed to patriotic scholars eager to trace their regional traditions to Etruria rather than Rome, and it helped stimulate a general European renewal of interest in things Etruscan. The first fruits of the revival soon became apparent: In 1726 the Etruscan Academy was established in the city of Cortona, in central Italy, to encourage the study of the civilization. Two years later the first recorded excavations were begun in the spectacular cliff-top necropolis of Volterra (*pages 6-7*), one of the ancient world's wealthiest cities. Artifacts recovered from the site over the next 30 years filled private collections and museums all across Europe, including modern Volterra's Guarnacci Museum, which became the world's first public Etruscan collection when it opened in 1761.

By then, a new word, Etruscheria, had been coined to describe the vogue for studying the culture, and both polite society and scholars were starting to show an interest. Indeed, well-heeled visitors toasted the ancients at picnics held among the tombs. And so-called Etruscan vases—many of which had actually been made in Greece and imported by rich Etruscans—became so popular the English potter Josiah Wedgwood chose the name Etruria for the new manufacturing center in the English Midlands that was to make him famous *(page 153)*.

The outbreak of the Napoleonic Wars at the end of the 18th century temporarily disrupted access to the Etruscan sites, but with the restoration of peace in 1815 a new period of archaeological activity dawned. In practically no time, Etruscan artifacts again flooded Europe's antique markets. As a matter of fact, so much pottery came from a necropolis discovered in 1828 at the town of Vulci, about 50 miles northwest of Rome, that even today a majority of the surviving vases can be traced to it.

In 1836 two amateur archaeologists unearthed a treasure in gold and amber objects buried in the tomb of an unknown noblewoman at Cerveteri, the site of the ancient city of Caere, 20 miles northwest of Rome. News of the discovery spread quickly around Europe. Together with colorful scenes of music, banqueting, hunting, and fishing found painted on the walls of the tombs at Tarquinia, an important Etruscan town 12 miles north of Civitavecchia first investigated in the 18th century, the artifacts confirmed a general impression of Etruria as a land of vitality and naturalness, as well as one of mystery and hidden riches.

The combination of wild and beautiful scenery and sequestered burial places was guaranteed to appeal to the sensibilities of the romantic era, then in its heyday. It was a time when young enthusiasts happily braved the primitive inns and endemic malaria that marked the region to comb wild gorges and picturesque ruins for traces of the lost civilization. One such explorer was George Dennis, a lowly clerk in the Excise Office in London. A self-taught classicist, he devoted his spare time to the investigation of Etruria and its antiquities and then wrote *The Cities and Cemeteries of Etruria*, a comprehensive two-volume overview of all the known sites. Published in 1848 and revised three times, the work sadly failed to win

Dennis either fame or fortune, but it attracted a small, discriminating readership—and has continued to do so, having attained the status of a classic. "Still the best single guide to Etruscan cities and tombs," the American art historian and archaeologist Nancy Thomson de Grummond has written of his work, "it is also important today because it gives reliable, precious information about monuments which have since been lost."

Dennis's book marked both the culmination of an age in which gifted and energetic amateurs worked to revive the memory of the Etruscans and the birth of the present era, in which professional archaeologists using increasingly sophisticated techniques set about trying to solve the many mysteries that surround the Etruscans. Much has been learned by reexamining the evidence uncovered in the initial, undisciplined burst of exploration. This has produced fewer spectacular finds than the first, but it has done more to extend knowledge of the people and their society. Scholars, for instance, now

In this photo, taken around 1920, a marble statue of Mario Guarnacci (left), completed in 1867, overlooks a room of Etruscan tufa and alabaster urns for cremated remains in Volterra's Guarnacci Museum. The containers, once described by writer D. H. Lawrence as "curiously attractive and alive," are part of an extensive Etruscan collection, founded by Guarnacci in 1761 as the first public museum devoted to Etruscan artifacts.

know enough to divide Etruscan history into five phases, four of which traditionally take the names of corresponding eras in Greek art history *(pages 158-159)*.

Experts can also piece together the basics of how the dead Etruscan language was written and spoken. Lacking the abundance of texts available to students of Greece and Rome, Etruscologists have had to glean as much information as possible from the seven centuries' worth of inscriptions that the Etruscans left on the tablets, boundary markers, hand mirrors, vases, sarcophagi, coins, and other items recovered so far. By comparing these with inscriptions on various ancient artifacts, scholars have deduced that the Etruscans learned the art of writing from Greek traders in the eighth century BC and that the alphabet they used was a version of the Greek one. There are indications that when the alphabet first arrived, it was regarded as something of a status symbol; objects from wealthy tombs were sometimes decorated with the new letters, indicating that they had prestige, and perhaps even magical significance.

As the Greek and Etruscan languages were in no way related, the alphabet needed some modification to make it a suitable vehicle for the Etruscan tongue, which linguists have described as both a soft burr and full of clicks and hisses. The symbols for exclusively Greek sounds were dropped, and new ones were introduced. Then the altered version was passed on to other Italian peoples—most importantly the Romans, who subsequently carried it to much of western Europe, where it remains in use even today. As a result, the Etruscans are to thank for the fact that the alphabet starts with the letters *a, b,* and *c,* rather than alpha, beta, and gamma. Meanwhile, a second channel of transmission, via the inhabitants of northern Italy across the Alps to the Germanic tribes of Europe, resulted in the development of runes, the script used by Scandinavian peoples.

The similarities between the Greek and Etruscan alphabets have meant that spelling out Etruscan words and deciphering their approximate meaning have never presented major problems. Scholars have been able to do so since the 18th century. One of the pieces they deciphered came to light under decidedly odd circumstances. The sequence of events began in Egypt in the late 1840s, when a Croatian nobleman named Mihael de Baric bought a mummy—then quite freely available—from an Alexandria antique dealer. Baric, an archivist at the royal chancellery of the Hungarian court, took his purchase back to his home in Vienna, where he proudly put it on dis-

The Etruscan alphabet girds the belly of a late-seventh-century-BC rooster-shaped vase or ink stand from Viterbo. Although the Etruscans did not use the letters b, d, g *(resembling a modern* c *here), or* o, *these letters do appear in the model alphabet that the Etruscans received from the Greeks* (bottom) *and then modified for their own purposes.*

play in his drawing room alongside curiosities and artworks obtained on previous world travels.

For a while, the mummy stood upright in a display case, its bandages still tightly wrapped around its head and stiff body. But at some point Baric must have partially unwound the fabric for the titillation of his nephew, who later reported gazing upon what he described as a childlike face. By the time that Baric died, in 1859, the mummy had been unwrapped completely, exposing the remains of a woman about 30 years old, and the body and the bandages were now conserved in separate cases. Baric's heirs presented both to the Egyptian section of the National Museum in Zagreb, where they arrived in late July 1862.

There the keeper of the collection, Professor Heinrich Karl Brugsch, immediately noticed something unusual about the linen bandages: One side was covered with writing in a language that the scholar was unable to identify. "I would never have discovered the writing on the wrappings if one of the bandages was not unrolled and showed its inside," Brugsch wrote in 1891. "My surprise at seeing that writing, which was unknown to me, was quite naturally great, and since I hoped to have found an Egyptian inscription either large or small, I therefore started to unroll what there was to unroll—which was done without much difficulty—and brought to light the mysterious text."

Even though an 1870 museum catalog states that the professor devoted years to the study of the inscriptions, their identity eluded him forever. According to the publication, they remained "of such novelty that they are without equal in the world."

Two more decades would pass before the riddle was finally solved. In 1891 the bandages were sent to the University of Vienna, where experts quickly identified the mystery language as Etruscan. The linen on which it was written was compact and tightly woven, and although it had been stained by blood and unguents, it seemed likely that it had been specially prepared in order to make the ink clearly legible. The text was neatly inscribed in two colors: black for the words themselves, and red for underlining and for a number of vertical lines that divided the text into nine-inch-wide columns. The investigators had little doubt as to the importance of the discovery: The Zagreb mummy wrappings were evidently scraps of the world's only surviving Etruscan book, preserved by chance by the mummification process.

Based upon close examination of the shapes of individual letters, the writing was dated to about 150 BC, though recent radiocarbon dating of the linen suggests it might be 200 years older. It contained no clues to indicate how the book had originally reached Egypt, though scholars have speculated that it might have been a possession of an Etruscan exile working in the service of the pharaohs. Once there, it apparently fell into the hands of mummifiers, who cut it up and used the strips as so much linen bandaging with which to wrap a corpse.

A religious work, the book lists the rituals to be offered to various gods on different days of the year. In its present form it contains 216 lines of text—substantially less than early accounts implied, indicating that sections may have been lost or given away in the years after its discovery. Scholars have also detected errors in the copying, possibly suggesting that the language was already falling into disuse when the book was written.

Though without question a boon to the study of the Etruscan language, the writing on the Zagreb mummy cloth proved to be less enlightening than its discoverers had initially hoped. Like most inscriptions, which take the form of tombstone carvings that simply give the name, and occasionally the title, of the deceased, the vocabulary employed contained too many repeated phrases and an excess of proper nouns to increase by many the 300 words that had already been deciphered.

So progress in reading Etruscan—that is, in expanding the vocabulary and in clarifying the rules of its grammar—has been slow. To speed things up, scholars have hoped to find a bilingual text pairing something written in Etruscan with the same passage translated into a known language. They require, in other words, an Etruscan equivalent to Egypt's Rosetta stone, discovered by Napoleon's army in 1799. The slab's parallel bands of Greek and Egyptian inscriptions provided the key to the deciphering of hieroglyphics.

Understandably, then, excitement grew in 1964 when it seemed that just such a text had been discovered. The find was made

Portions of a religious calendar, the only known Etruscan book in existence, survive in strips (top). Egyptian mummifiers used the linen book to wrap the body of a 30-year-old woman (bottom), now known as the Zagreb mummy for the museum in Croatia where she and her unusual wrappings eventually came to rest in 1862.

24

near the imposing medieval castle of Santa Severa, on the Tyrrhenian coast about 30 miles northwest of Rome. In antiquity the site was known as Pyrgi, after the Greek word for towers, and was home to the principal port serving Caere, eight miles inland. Roman writers knew the harbor well. The epic poet Virgil referred to "ancient Pyrgi," and a fourth-century-AD editor of his work described it as "a fairly well-known stronghold during the age when the Etruscans practiced the trade of piracy"—the seventh and sixth centuries BC.

The ill-gotten rewards of the trade were obviously great, for the town's temple was renowned for the richness of its endowment. The sanctuary's reputation even tempted Dionysius the Elder, the ruler of the Greek colony of Syracuse on Sicily. After a famous raid staged in 384 BC, Dionysius made off with 1,000 talents from the temple treasury—an amount so enormous it equaled the total indemnity he was forced to pay after losing a war against the Carthaginians four years later.

Remains of the temple were revealed by chance in the course of a coastal land-reclamation scheme in 1956, when power-driven plows turning the earth about 450 yards from the castle churned up tiles and terra-cotta works dating to Etruscan times. The plowing was halted after the doyen of Etruscan scholars, Massimo Pallottino, a professor of Etruscology and Italic antiquities at the University of Rome, inspected the site. Excavation began the following year under

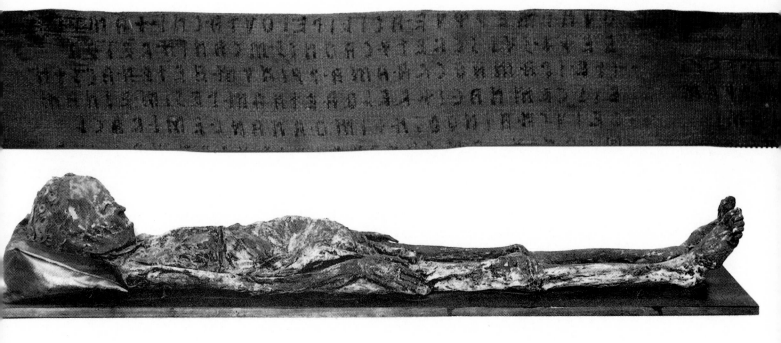

Pallottino's general supervision and the close direction of Giovanni Colonna, who was at that time an assistant to Pallottino.

During seven campaigns conducted between 1957 and 1964, the excavators uncovered the remains of two temples—one built between 480 and 470 BC, the other around 500 BC—linked by a small rectangular enclosure. It was in this space, near a sacrificial well containing the bones of an ox, a piglet, a badger, and a cock, that the most exciting find of the entire project was to be unearthed in the final year's digging.

Pietro Giovanni Guzzo, now the archaeological superintendent of Italy's Emilia-Romagna region, was then a young Etruscology student spending his second summer working at the site. Early on July 8, he left his tent on the beach and resumed the task that had occupied him and a dozen or so other students for two sweltering days—brushing and scraping away the dirt that covered the rectangular area. Until then, the painstaking work had yielded nothing more than small pottery sherds, but when one of the students reached a depth of about 20 inches, he uncovered something unusual: three thin gold sheets, each measuring 7½ by 3½ inches, that had been folded and buried, apparently for safekeeping.

"They looked to me like three omelets, rolled up like that," Guzzo recalled. "We knew they were gold because of their yellow color, but they did not glint because the earth was wet and they had a film on them. It's always exciting when you find something, but we had no idea of their importance. I did a sketch—we did not have a camera—and then the chief of the workmen, a very expert man from Cerveteri called Oreste Brandolini, said we should remove them for safety. They were picked up and put in plastic bags with numbers to show their position."

Neither Pallottino nor Colonna was on site at the time, but Colonna arrived shortly afterward. With a camera in hand, he or-

The folded Pyrgi plaques lie in their excavation trench (above), *replaced there for this historic July 8, 1964, photograph shortly after their initial discovery and removal. The 7½-by-3½-inch gold sheets at right—two in Etruscan* (near right and center) *and one in Phoenician* (far right)—*record the dedication of a cult center to a Phoenician goddess by an Etruscan ruler. The tablets, from around 500 BC, have proved valuable in the study of religion and history and have contributed much to scholars' understanding of the Etruscan language.*

dered the tablets returned to where they had been found. Then he took the now-famous photograph that accompanied his official account of the discovery.

When the plaques were gingerly unfolded, they were found to contain inscriptions recording the dedication of a sanctuary to a goddess by Thefarie Velianas, the ruler of Caere. Twenty-nine golden-headed nails had been folded in with the sheets, suggesting that they had originally been posted, probably on the door of one of the temples. The texts had presumably been hidden to preserve them from plundering enemy forces—conceivably even from those of Dionysius of Syracuse, though there is no way of confirming the possibility. Two of the inscriptions were in Etruscan, but the third was in Phoenician. Here at last, it seemed, was the long-sought key to the remaining problems of Etruscan.

In fact, the Pyrgi plaques proved to be of only limited use as a bilingual. The longer of the two Etruscan inscriptions ran to just 37 words, and the Phoenician text turned out to be not a literal, word-for-word translation of the Etruscan, but a separate piece of writing that merely described the same topics as the Etruscan. Nonetheless, scholars accustomed to reading only funerary inscriptions rejoiced to finally have one with historical content. And as Pallottino wrote, the correspondence between the Phoenician inscription and the longer of the two Etruscan inscriptions "constitutes an enormous step forward in our knowledge of the vocabulary and structure of the Etruscan language."

Such a stride, however, has done little to address a much larger uncertainty concerning the origins of the language, for unlike Greek, Celtic as spoken by the tribes of Gaul, Latin, or most other known early Italian tongues, Etruscan does not belong to the Indo-European language family. Indeed, attempts to link it with any other known tongue have proved unsuccessful. And it is this apparent uniqueness of the Etruscan language that has lent an aura of mystery to the Etruscan people.

French archaeologists working on the Aegean island of Lem-

Though the voices are mostly silent, the faces of the Etruscan people and their gods, such as those below, have been preserved. Among them are, from left to right, a middle-aged noble, a hooded child from Vulci, a solemn-faced youth, a woman from Cerveteri, the goddess Uni, and a man from Etruria's final days.

nos in 1885 found a stele, subsequently dated to the sixth century BC, that bore a figure of a spear-carrying warrior. A carved 33-word inscription in a language that closely resembled Etruscan ran around the piece. Almost half a century later, Italians working on the island uncovered pottery sherds bearing fragmentary inscriptions apparently in the same tongue—Etruscan's only known relative. Scholars think the language may have been used on the island before its conquest by Athens in the latter half of the sixth century BC, after which time Greek gradually came to replace it. However, what its connections were with the tongue spoken in Etruria, 700 miles to the west, remains unresolved.

Such uncertainties are inextricably enmeshed with the larger question of the origins of Etruscan civilization as a whole. The de-

bate on this subject goes back to the Greek historian Herodotus, who wrote in the fifth century BC. He claimed that long ago the Lydians—neighbors of the Greeks inhabiting what is now mainland Turkey—experienced a famine that endured for 18 years. At first they tried to cope with the hardship by eating only on alternate days, devoting the ones in between to continuous play, using dice, ball games, and other pastimes to distract them from their hunger. When this proved unworkable, the king ordered his people to draw lots, dividing them into two groups. One remained in Lydia; the other, under the command of the ruler's son Tyrrhenus, set off in ships to seek a better livelihood elsewhere. "They passed many countries and finally reached Umbria in the north of Italy," the historian concluded, "where they settled and still live to this day. Here they changed their name from Lydians to Tyrrhenians, after the king's son Tyrrhenus, who was their leader."

The story had much to recommend it to Greeks of Herodotus's day, who considered the Etruscans they met in Italy as alien as the Lydians they knew in their homeland; both peoples, to Greek eyes, shared a reputation for high living and low morals. For more recent observers too the story has had superficial attractions. The idea of an armada of invading immigrants would neatly explain

A 1989 reconstruction of a Villanovan wattle-and-daub hut stands in Bologna's Margherita Gardens. The architects based interior structure and wall materials on site findings such as postholes (below) *and wall channels and impressions of reeds, straw, and twigs left in remnants of clay wall packing. Hut-shaped urns suggested exterior design, including the smoke vent and geometric patterns. Builders also studied similar huts still being constructed by shepherds just decades ago.*

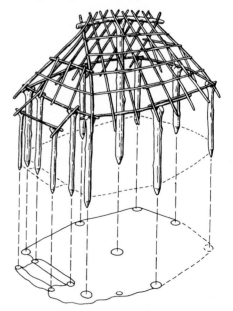

the distinctive qualities of Etruscan civilization, as exemplified especially by their language. Indeed, it was once suggested that while Tyrrhenus made his westward voyage, he may have deposited some of his people on Lemnos.

There is evidence also that the Etruscans themselves saw their history as starting from a fixed point of the type a sudden irruption into a new land might represent. They counted their history in units called saecula, or ages, and expected only 10 to pass between their rise and fall. The length of a saeculum seems to have been determined by the life span of the longest-lived member of each generation. Consequently, experts cannot work out precisely the starting date from which the Etruscans measured their history but suspect that it fell sometime in the 11th or 10th century BC.

Plausible as it might seem at first sight, most scholars now discount Herodotus's theory, since Etruscan civilization betrayed no Lydian traits. Though a strong Eastern influence was to make itself felt, it took the form of borrowings from Syria, from the Phoenicians, and above all from the Greeks. And in the matter of language, no known link exists between Etruscan and Lydian, which belongs to the Indo-European family.

As Herodotus's version has fallen out of favor, increasing attention has been paid to an alternative view put forward in classical times by Dionysius of Halicarnassus. Dionysius wrote a history of Rome that sought to prove—inaccurately, as scholars now know—that the Romans were of Greek origin. In pursuit of his thesis, he distinguished the Roman people from their Etruscan neighbors, whom he considered fairly evidently un-Greek, not to say alien. But instead of tracing the Etruscans' roots to Lydia, he maintained that they were an autochthonous, or indigenous, people. "The nation migrated from nowhere else," he wrote, "but was native to the country, since it is found to be a very ancient nation and to agree with no other in its language or in its manner of living." In other words, the Etruscans were aboriginal Italians.

In the absence of written records to throw light on the conflicting claims, students of Etruscology have had to turn to archaeology for clarification. Though the results of two centuries of digging have been ambiguous enough to allow for different interpretations of the evidence, a consensus view is emerging.

The archaeological record shows central Italy to have been relatively undeveloped for much of the second millennium BC. Although the population grew steadily over the centuries, people continued to live in simple hillside agricultural settlements whose lack of fortifications suggests an absence of external menaces.

Change evidently came in the late Bronze Age, from roughly 1300 to 1000 BC. Though scholars have not discerned an abrupt break in history's thread, the settlements were abandoned and larger, fortified centers began to develop. By that time, burial customs had changed and cremation had become the norm. Archaeologists have also discovered objects from the eastern Mediterranean dating to this period, indicating that trade links of some kind existed.

Proponents of the view that the Etruscans migrated to Etruria cite these finds in support of their argument. And indisputably, a time of troubles did befall the Mediterranean world around the year 1200 BC, when many peoples were on the move. Unknown assailants overwhelmed the Hittite realm in Turkey, and the Mycenaean culture in Greece crumbled. Even Egypt, with nearly two millennia of Pharaonic rule behind it, was severely threatened and was saved only by victory in one of history's first recorded naval encounters, fought against an enemy referred to as the Sea Peoples by Ramses III. Historians still dispute the identity of these boat-borne invaders, though the Philistines—Goliath's people, the future foes of the Israelites—are believed to have been among them.

If large-scale immigration into Etruria occurred at any stage, it was likely at this time. And if not the Lydians, some scholars argue, then another eastern Mediterranean people or peoples may have arrived in Italy, bringing with them new habits and a language that was different from their neighbors' in Europe. Their presence could account for the linguistic links suggested by the Lemnos stele. But then

Near Tarquinia, a pit burial of the late Villanovan period (above), excavated by Italian archaeologist Luigi Pernier in the early 1900s, lies partially exposed, a symbolic pottery helmet in the center. Most people of the Villanovan period cremated their dead and placed the urns in circular burial pits, often called pozzo (well) graves. Though some urns were hut shaped, most were biconical receptacles, covered by a pottery dish or helmet, or a more expensive helmet of bronze (right), probably honoring a warrior.

again, all evidence of East-West contact could equally well be ascribed to trade links.

What is certain is that by the 10th century BC, when the Bronze Age was gradually giving way to the Iron Age, an Etruscan culture had already established itself. Dating from approximately 1000 to 700 BC, this early phase of Etruscan history takes the title Villanovan from an estate on the outskirts of Bologna where artifacts produced during it were first identified in 1853. The property belonged to Count Giovanni Gozzadini, a wealthy amateur archaeologist who financed the excavation out of his own pocket. He and his helpers unearthed 193 tombs in all, containing funerary urns, bronze vessels, and other objects. Because the items were crafted in styles that were unfamiliar at the time, they caused considerable controversy. Scholars mistakenly argued that the pieces must have been the work of either Gauls or Greeks, but Gozzadini himself correctly identified them as early Etruscan work, and his judgment has been confirmed by posterity.

Subsequent excavations have uncovered Villanovan remains at many sites in the Etruscan heartland, and also as far afield as Campania, south of Rome. The settlements tend to coincide with later Etruscan cities, encouraging the notion that Etruscan civilization progressed from its early to later phases without interruption. The picture that emerges is one of Iron Age farmers living in oval or rectangular huts made of clay, reeds, and wood that were grouped into small villages. These people, who are known as proto-Etruscans, were skillful metalworkers, and they produced functional though coarsely executed pottery. They preserved the ashes of the dead in pottery urns and sometimes in clay containers charmingly modeled to resemble the huts in which they lived *(page 30)*. And though they possessed iron, they still made many of their tools and weapons of bronze.

This peaceful, rural world changed radically in the eighth century BC as a result of one of history's great economic upheavals. In a few decades—a period that one recent historian has described as the most important time in Etruscan history—groups of adjacent villages amalgamated into city-states. These larger settlements, scholars speculate, made it easier for the Etruscans to do business with the

traders who were crisscrossing the Mediterranean. Among them were the Phoenicians.

Famous mariners and traders from the Mediterranean's eastern shores, the Phoenicians had settlements on the island of Sardinia by early in the ninth century BC and, according to tradition, had founded the colony of Carthage on the coast of present-day Tunisia in 814 BC. Etruria's bountiful minerals would certainly have attracted additional settlers to the Etruscan lands as well, had the local inhabitants not repulsed potential colonists. The reputation for piracy that Etruscan sailors were to acquire was no doubt a reflection of the fierceness of the resistance they offered.

Within a half century the Greeks also arrived, and their influence quickly outweighed even that of the Phoenicians. In fact, the encounter between Greeks and Etruscans proved crucial not just for the history of Etruria or Italy but for Western civilization as a whole, because their relations formed the bridge through which the civilization of the classical world first reached western Europe. The Greeks gained their foothold in the region on the island of Ischia in the bay of Naples.

They knew the place as Pithecusae, perhaps from the word *pithecos*, meaning monkey; Pithecusae presumably meant "monkey island." There Greeks from the Aegean island of Euboea established their first trading post in the second quarter of the eighth century BC. The Euboeans had already established a similar center at Al Mina on the coast of what is now Syria, so they were well placed to introduce the Etruscans not just to their own culture but also to the already ancient civilization of the Middle Eastern lands. Indeed, Pithecusae seems to have been frequented by merchants not only from Greece but also from other eastern Mediterranean nations: Excavations conducted on the island since 1952 under the direction of the Italian archaeologist Giorgio Buchner have turned up locally made pottery with inscriptions in such exotic tongues as Phoenician and Aramaic, the lingua franca of the Near East during the seventh and sixth centuries BC.

Digging in the island's cemetery, on its acropolis, or citadel, and in a suburban industrial quarter, Buchner has also discovered ample evidence of an acquisitive, creative, and literate society. Finds include a locally made wine bowl decorated with a shipwreck scene,

believed to be the earliest example of pictorial narrative art found on Italian soil, and a drinking vessel whose rim bears an inscription in Greek that reads, "Nestor had a most drinkworthy cup, but whoever drinks of mine will straightaway be smitten with desire of fair-crowned Aphrodite"—the goddess of love. The text refers to a celebrated cup mentioned in Homer's *Iliad,* making the inscription not merely one of the first-known intimations of the amorous potential of alcohol but also one of the world's earliest literary allusions.

At Pithecusae, Buchner has recovered Phoenician vases, scarab amulets from Egypt, and an ointment flask and seals produced in Syria, suggesting the extensive range of cultural contacts the base opened to the Etruscans and neighboring peoples. Equally important, if less aesthetically attractive, was the iron slag unearthed on the acropolis's ancient rubbish dump, as well as two rough pots that,

Survivors of a capsized ship swim for safety (above), *while the bodies of the less fortunate float nearby, one poor victim's head in the jaws of an enormous fish. This scene comes from Pithecusae's famous shipwreck krater* (left), *an eighth-century-BC artifact reconstructed from scattered pottery fragments found at the site of the Greek settlement on the island of Ischia, opposite today's Naples.*

35

judging from the slag encrusted on their bases, must have been used as crucibles. Experts have taken these finds as conclusive proof that iron foundries existed on the island, confirming the view that the settlement was originally established to provide access to Etruscan minerals. Indeed, Buchner wrote, "There can be little doubt that with the possession of the base of Al Mina in the East and that of Pithecusae in the West, the Euboeans were, from about 775 to about 700 BC, the masters of the trade between the Eastern Mediterranean and Central Italy."

As a conduit for Greek culture, Pithecusae exerted immense influence on the Etruscans. Evidence from their tombs indicates that the amount of imported wares surged and that local artisans rapidly imitated the foreign styles and techniques. With trade flourishing, new wealth flowed into Etruria and encouraged the growth of bigger and more elaborate cities. Burial patterns, however, suggest that the riches were not evenly spread. Whereas all Etruscans had previously enjoyed relative equality in death, now elaborate and costly interments of warriors in full armor appeared, suggesting the emergence of an aristocratic class. Such innovations as writing and wine drinking were also introduced.

By the end of the eighth century BC, Etruscan civilization had been largely transformed. The simple Villanovan farming society had been replaced by a more sophisticated world: that of the elegant, pleasure-loving aristocrats whose languorous, reclining images are preserved in tomb paintings. The Greeks had brought aspects of civilization to Etruscan society and had vastly increased its scope and ambitions. Etruria was about to enter a new phase of expansion. And while its people would move from their city-states across much of mainland Italy, the influence of its new arts and knowledge would ultimately traverse the Western world.

THE JOYOUS MUSIC OF LIFE

The laughter has died away, the pipes are still, and the patter of feet dancing in the dust has faded into the silence. Yet thanks to the artists of Etruria, the modern world can see Etruscans at play and partake of their fun in the wall paintings decorating many of their tombs.

These lively images apparently served not only as reminders of the occupants' accomplishments and happiness on earth, but also as expressions of the Etruscan belief that similar pleasures would be found in the afterlife. Among other things, they show dancers and musicians, such as the lyre player above from Tarquinia's Tomb of the Leopards, entertaining at lavish banquets, athletes testing their skills at funeral games, and charioteers racing to the finish line. Only much later in Etruria's history, when death ceased to be viewed as simply an extension of life and was seen instead as an anxious journey to a fearsome underworld, did the wall paintings begin to take on a more melancholy tone. Yet if one quality can be said to mark the art of these life-loving people, it is its vitality, a sense of laughing in the face of death.

After the underground tombs were hollowed out of the volcanic rock of the Etruscan countryside, plasterers coated the interiors with a mixture of calcium carbonate and clay (turf was sometimes added to prevent the plaster from hardening before the application of the paint). The walls were then covered with a neutral color on which artists drew their outlines before applying colors. These were derived from natural sources: yellow from iron; red from iron oxide; blue from ground lapis lazuli; green from a combination of malachite, copper, calcium, and flint. Lamp soot or charcoal was used as a source of black. By diluting and mixing these primary colors, the artists created a rainbow of hues for their dynamic compositions, depicting scenes taken from favorite myths and legends or derived from the rich experience of living.

A naked boy plummets headlong into the sea in this sixth-century-BC fresco from Tarquinia's Tomb of Hunting and Fishing (right). The realistic rendering of the figure suggests that the artist actually studied his subject for the painting, perhaps by watching divers as they plunged into the Tyrrhenian Sea.

Two teams of horses race for the finish in this fifth-century-BC tomb painting from Chiusi. The charioteers have tied the reins around their waists in order to quickly maneuver turns, a dangerous practice that was eventually adopted by the Romans.

A young beardless wrestler locks his older opponent in a firm grip in this detail from the Tomb of the Augurs painted in Tarquinia around 530 BC. The Etruscans' love for sporting events is evident in the many depictions of athletic contests in Etruscan art, from tomb paintings to bronze figurines.

As a bird flutters toward a tree (perhaps to escape the cat at lower right), a couple abandon themselves to music. This fresco and others from the fifth-century-BC Tomb of the Triclinium—considered one of the finest in Tarquinia—have been removed from the walls in order to prevent further deterioration.

Painted in vibrant colors, a youth plays the double pipe in this detail (right) from Tarquinia's early fifth-century-BC Tomb of the Leopards. A favorite instrument of the Etruscans, the double pipe took some dexterity to play since the musician fingered a pipe in each hand.

Velia Seitithi—the wife of Larth Velchi, an important member of the priesthood in the third century BC—tenderly offers her husband an egg, symbol of immortality, in this detail of a banquet scene from the Tomb of the Shields at Tarquinia. Though dressed in their best finery and partaking of an extravagant banquet, the couple's mood is somber and indicates the Etruscans' changing attitude toward death.

The noble class's taste for luxury and pleasure is evident in this mural from the Tomb of the Leopards, one of the most impressive in Tarquinia. Men and women (the women are depicted with fair complexions) wear festive crowns of myrtle leaves in their hair and recline in comfort on a banquet couch while being waited upon by servants. The ravages of time and tourism have taken their toll of the fresco and the lower part of the painting has been destroyed.

A HAPPY IDYLL IN ETRUSCAN HISTORY

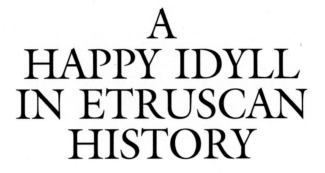

In 1961 a party of photographers and spear fishermen made what was expected to be a routine dive off Giglio, an island south of Elba about 10 miles from the coast of Etruria. They were students at a diving school set up that year by a Londoner named Reg Vallintine, who was leading the excursion. Vallintine described what happened next in a magazine article, "Over a dividing ridge we went and suddenly on the sandy valley below us were mysterious scattered objects and amphorae." The discovery excited Vallintine and his companions, but at the time they had no notion of just how important it was. They had come upon part of the cargo of the oldest deep-sea ship yet found—a merchantman plying the Etruscan coast around 600 BC, when the cities of Etruria were in their commercial and political heyday.

The wreck soon became an attraction for divers on the island. Many took away souvenirs of their visit. Vallintine grew sufficiently concerned about the gradual disappearance of the objects still lying on the seabed to cover the site with sand when he left Giglio a couple of years later to pursue his career elsewhere. For almost two decades, the 2,500-year-old vessel would be lost once more.

But the items taken from the ship survived, and one of them was to spark the interest of a young Oxford don with a passion for underwater exploration. Mensun Bound had been born in the Falk-

Etruscan sailors, transformed by Dionysius into dolphins, dive into the water on this vase. The vessel, dating to about 500 BC, is among the earliest representations of one of several legends that link Etruscans to the neighboring seas.

land Islands. He had spent an adventurous youth crewing on a tramp steamer in the South Atlantic before working his way through college in New York and graduating with first-class honors. He then moved to England, and in London in 1981 he picked up the trail that led him to the Giglio wreck.

At the time his mind was on an entirely different project: the salvaging of the *Mary Rose*, a four-masted English warship that sank between the Isle of Wight and Portsmouth during a battle in 1545. Its raising was one of the largest marine archaeology projects of the day. While visiting the diver responsible for locating the Tudor boat, Bound noticed an amphora handle displayed as an ornament on the man's bookshelves. The object was obviously ancient, and Bound recognized its shape as distinctively Etruscan. His interest was immediately aroused, for up to that time no Etruscan wrecks had officially been located.

The diver told him about the Giglio discovery and put him in touch with Vallintine. What the Londoner told Bound about the sunken vessel convinced him that it deserved further investigation. But to raise money to finance such a project, he needed firm evidence of its historical importance. With the aid of Vallintine's notes and some old photographs, he set about tracking down further objects that had been removed from the site 20 years before.

Mensun Bound (above, left), *director of the underwater excavation that retrieved objects from the so-called Giglio wreck, and Reg Vallintine, chief diver, carefully brush silt from the wooden keel of the ship. Little natural light penetrates the darkness at this extreme depth, forcing the team to use powerful flash and strobe lights to illuminate the work surface.*

The trail led all around Europe. One geometrically patterned vase eventually located in Monte Carlo dated from 600 BC. The most exciting piece of all, a bronze helmet engraved with a design of boars and a two-headed snake, was believed to be in the possession of a German known only by his Christian name, Hans. Through patient detective work among fellow divers, Bound discovered the man's surname and traced him to an address in Hamburg. He still had the helmet, safely stored in a bank vault, and he permitted Bound to examine and photograph it.

The data Bound gathered proved sufficiently convincing to attract funding from Oxford University and other sources, and the young professor eventually mounted a full-scale expedition. Vallintine was appointed its chief diver, and on a reconnaissance trip in 1982 he was able, with some difficulty, to relocate the site he had last seen almost two decades ago. The ship lay 150 feet down at the foot of a reef—the same one that had evidently caused its ruin two and a half millennia before.

Up to 120 volunteers assisted with the excavation of the wreck, which took four summers. The ship turned out to have been carrying a mixed cargo, including a supply of cigar-shaped anchor stocks, the heavy crosspiece at the top of the anchor. The stocks were made of stone quarried locally on Giglio; it was presumably after picking up this consignment that the vessel had come to grief. Other goods aboard included furniture, weaponry, metal ingots, perfume containers, and painted pottery from the city of Corinth, an ancient commercial capital of the Greek world. There was also a considerable quantity of pitch, used at the time both as a sealant and as a flavoring for retsina-type wine. The sticky resin had leaked onto the seabed, solidifying around some of the objects and so helping to preserve them.

Some of the discoveries had considerable historical significance. Pipes taken from the wreck permitted scholars from the University of Florence's Conservatory of Music to replicate the Etruscan musical scale for the

Hammered from a single sheet of bronze, this exquisitely engraved Corinthian-style helmet from the Giglio wreck is a masterpiece of Greek metalwork. Despite its beauty, the helmet still had a functional purpose—to protect its owner during battle.

first time. Pits found in some of the amphorae indicated that the ship was carrying olives or olive oil, even though olive trees had not previously been recorded in Italy at such an early date.

The climax of the excavation came in 1985, when a 10-foot length of the keel was successfully raised. It was determined that the main components of the ship had been bonded together with cord, a technique known as sewn construction. The discovery increased the likelihood that the merchantman might be an Etruscan vessel rather than a trader from Greece, where mortise and tenon joints were usually employed at the time. But to this day, no one can say for sure which port its sailors called home.

The years around 600 BC when the ship went down saw the power of the Etruscan city-states at a peak. Emigrants pushed out of their homeland between the Arno and Tiber Rivers on the Tyrrhenian side of Italy, both across the Apennines to the Adriatic and into the region south of Rome known today as Campania. And in 616 BC, the Etruscan-born Lucius Tarquinius Priscus was named the first Tarquin king of Rome, then nothing more than an amorphous collection of settlements along the Tiber River. Under his rule, and that of his Etruscan successors Servius Tullius and Tarquinius Superbus, a swampy area that later became the Forum was drained, foundations were laid for the Eternal City's first sewer system, and temples—including one of the great landmarks of Rome, the Temple of Jupiter—rose where only huts had stood before.

For the coastal city-states at least, the basis of Etruscan greatness was firmly rooted in sea power. The Greeks—both partners and rivals of the new power—spoke grudgingly of an Etruscan thalassocracy, meaning rule of the sea, and accused the city-states of piracy, no doubt partly because they were so adept at guarding their own coasts. The historian Strabo, writing some six centuries later, even claimed that "men were so afraid of the pirate vessels of the Tyrrhenians and the savagery of the barbarians in this region that they would not so much as sail there for trading."

Strabo, as scholars now know, was wrong. Greek, Phoenician, and other traders during this time were pouring into those Etruscan cities that were accessible to the sea—such as Tarquinia and, later, Caere—offering exquisite artifacts of gold and silver and ivory and bronze for the Etruscans' metals and finished goods. An exam-

48

pieces—called bucchero *sottile* (thin)—have extremely fine walls and a high, metallic sheen, possibly achieved using a refined slip and extensive burnishing. Designs were usually incised, as on the late-seventh-century-BC pitcher (with a 19th-century stand) at left, on which a figure rides two horselike creatures.

By the sixth century BC, artisans in Chiusi and Orvieto were turning out a thicker, less lustrous ware known as bucchero *pesante* (heavy). Low reliefs supplanted delicate incising. On the oinochoe above, a rolled cylinder rendered the scene of Perseus preparing to cut off Medusa's head.

Production of the black pottery ended about 200 years after it had begun. Yet bucchero's beauty and unique characteristics have made it the national pottery of Etruria.

ple of just how fabulously rich trade was making the early Italians came vividly to light in 1836, when a forgotten repository, the Regolini-Galassi Tomb, offered up one of the most spectacular gold hoards ever discovered.

The tomb—located near Cerveteri, the ancient site of Caere—took its name from its discoverers, Father Alessandro Regolini, a local priest, and General Vincenzo Galassi, a retired soldier. Excavating at the periphery of a circular burial site that measured more than 150 feet in diameter and had once been topped by an impressive tumulus, Regolini found five different chambers, all of which had been stripped of their contents by graverobbers. Disappointed but far from defeated, the priest decided to sink a shaft at the midpoint of the burial site.

Hoping to locate an undisturbed sixth tomb, Regolini, to his surprise, broke through its ceiling. The chamber took the form of a passageway about 60 feet long and just four feet wide. The lower half of the tomb was hollowed out of the living rock, but the ceiling was vaulted in a rather primitive fashion, with overlapping stone slabs on each side gradually converging to leave a narrow channel topped by large blocks of stone. More than halfway along its length, the passage was interrupted by a doorway, which divided the tomb into an outer and inner chamber.

A bronze couch bearing powdery human remains rested in the outer room, and the remnants of a four-wheeled wooden funeral wagon, decorated with bronze, stood nearby. An iron sword, 10 javelins, and eight ceremonial shields indicated that the deceased had been a warrior. On either side of the outer room, near the doorway, Regolini found two small oval compartments that had been hollowed out of the rock, possibly sometime after the rest of the tomb had been constructed. The first held a pottery urn filled with human ashes; the second was a depository for various bronze and iron vessels. One of the pots, Regolini's workers discovered, contained lumps of a resinous substance that turned out to be incense. When a small piece was lighted, it produced smoke so thick and pungent that everyone was forced out of the tomb.

Although these discoveries were exceptional, even more dramatic finds awaited the archaeologist in the inner chamber, as the romantic-era traveler George Dennis related in his book *The Cities and Cemeteries of Etruria*. "Further in," he wrote, "stood two bronze caldrons for perfumes, as in the outer chamber: and then, at

Three nine-inch gold pendants, with lions' heads attached, decorate a necklace from the Regolini-Galassi Tomb. Each pendant is inset with amber that the Etruscans imported from the Baltic Sea, some 800 miles to the north.

the end of the tomb, on no couch, bier, or sarcophagus, not even on a rude bench of rock, but on the bare ground, lay—a corpse?—no, for it had ages since returned to dust, but a number of gold ornaments, whose position showed most clearly that, when placed in the tomb, they were upon a human body. The richness, beauty, and abundance of these articles, all of pure gold, were amazing—such a collection, it has been said, 'would not be found in the shop of a well-furnished goldsmith.' "

Among the treasures belonging to the occupant, a woman laid to rest years before the other two burials, were huge earrings, a pair of massive bracelets, necklaces, rings, a pendant, and a beautifully embossed breastplate, as well as 18 brooches, the largest nearly a foot long. Working in haste for fear of tomb robbers, the discoverer removed some 650 objects, including more than a basketful of golden fragments that experts believe had once adorned some kind of linen garment, long since deteriorated. General Galassi bought the artifacts and showed them for a time in his home. Then they were purchased by the Vatican and put on display.

The only clues to the identity of the tomb's occupants were the words Larthia and Mi Larthia scratched on three silver vessels. Linguists believe the inscriptions refer to the male Etruscan forename *Larth*—perhaps the man buried in the outer chamber—and should be translated as "I am of Larth."

Such discoveries make clear the type of luxury goods favored by the elite in seventh-century Etruria. The precious metals needed to make them were not available locally, nor were the ostrich eggs, faience, and additional artifacts found in other tombs of the period. These items had to be imported from such faraway places as Egypt, North Syria, Assyria, Cyprus, and Asia Minor, as well as the Phoenician ports and Greece. Traders following a long-established overland route to northern Europe also brought amber from the Baltic to be used for jewelry and other forms of personal adornment.

Historians cannot describe the exact route by which each object found its way to Etruria (page 54), but it is certain the Phoenicians played an important role. Their traders, combining commercial acumen with great navigational skills, had been sailing for centuries from their homeland on the Mediterranean's eastern shore to the Strait of Gibraltar and beyond, carrying goods from western Asia to exchange for local produce or raw materials in the ports they visited.

Voyagers such as these no doubt carried away a good deal of Etruscan handiwork. By the seventh century BC, native schools of pottery, metalwork, sculpture, and painting had developed in Etruria's cities, and their products were distributed around much of the Mediterranean basin. Archaeologists have found quantities of Etruscan exports, especially bucchero, a black pottery, along the shores of the rest of Italy, on the islands of Sardinia and Sicily, and in southern France, Spain, North Africa, and Greece.

Scholars have hypothesized that aspects of Etruscan civilization also traveled north along trade routes to less developed European societies in what are today parts of northern Italy, Austria, and Slovenia. Though the new ways seem to have had relatively little impact on the peasant majority, members of the ruling class apparently were eager to adopt them as marks of their status. Evidence of this

The body of the warrior interred in the first chamber of the Regolini-Galassi Tomb was brought to the burial vault on this seventh-century wooden cart fitted with a bronze funerary couch. Its wood having disintegrated centuries ago, the bronze fittings decorating the sides of the cart and the iron wheel rims were all that remained of the vehicle to guide restorers in its reconstruction.

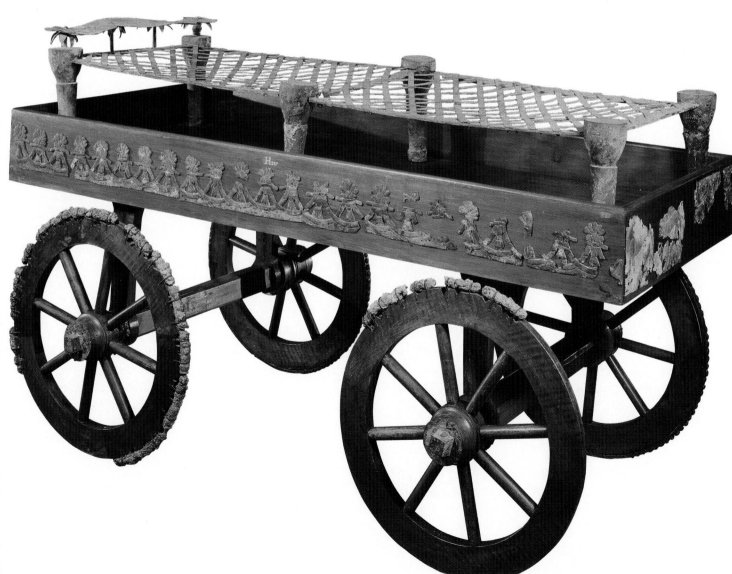

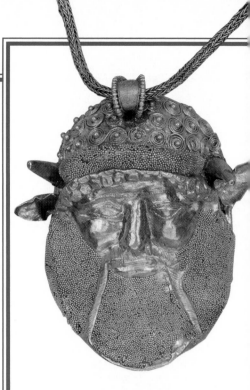

acculturation exists in the form of large, locally made bronze buckets called situlae.

Used by the so-called situla people to hold wine at banquets and discovered in the graves of their chiefs and warriors, some of the buckets were decorated with motifs that can be traced directly to Etruscan sources, such as a gory depiction of monsters devouring limbs. From Etruria also came a taste for organizing the decoration of the buckets in bands showing processions of people whose clothing, banquets, athletic contests, and method of fighting indicate Etruscan influence as well.

The first Greek artifacts appeared in Etruria early in the eighth century BC, carried there no doubt by a trickle of individual trading vessels. But when emigrants from the Greek island of Euboea founded Pithecusae on the island of Ischia in the Bay of Naples during the second quarter of the eighth century BC, the trickle quickly became a torrent. A commercial emporium not just for Euboeans but for traders from around the Mediterranean, the trading post proved to be a roaring success. Word of its prosperity spread quickly around the Greek world and attracted the interest of other settlers.

Within 50 years, permanent Greek colonies sprang up at half a dozen sites on the coasts of southern Italy and Sicily. The first was at Cumae, established around 740 BC less than 10 miles from Pithecusae on the mainland shore of the Bay of Naples. Syracuse and other parts of Sicily were settled over the next decade. Then Sybaris, which was to develop an overland trading route to the Etruscan cities, was founded on the instep of Italy around 720 BC. Taras, on the peninsula's heel, came 10 years later. By the century's end, the whole area was so thickly sown with Greek colonies that classical writers christened it Magna Graecia, or Great Greece.

Although the naval and military strength of the Etruscan cities prevented the Greeks from establishing colonies in Etruria itself, individual immigrants were allowed in and sometimes flourished. According to Dionysius of Halicarnassus, Demaratus, the father of the first Etruscan king of Rome, was a wealthy Greek merchant forced into exile by political intrigues in his home city of Corinth. He chose to settle in Etruria because of the trading links he already had with the place, and he brought along three artists whose Greek names speak of their talents: Eucheir, or "skilled hands"; Eugrammus, "skilled draftsman"; and Diopus, "user of the level." And, indeed, archaeologists have uncovered indicators that Greek artisans

A LOST TECHNIQUE FOUND AGAIN

Etruscan goldsmiths were masters of granulation, a technique that enabled them to fix hundreds of gold granules on jewelry such as the pendant above and the fibula, or pin, at right. The process originated in Mesopotamia more than 3,000 years ago and spread to Greece and to Etruria before dying out.

For centuries European goldsmiths unsuccessfully tried to recapture the lost art. Only in fairly recent times has it been re-created. Experiments carried out in 1992 at Murlo in Tuscany suggest that the Etruscans employed several methods for producing the beaded surfaces.

As nearly as can be determined, the jewelers cut gold wire into tiny segments and layered them between powdered charcoal in clay crucibles, then proceeded to heat the vessels in charcoal fires. As the temperature reached 2,012 degrees Fahrenheit, the gold melted into tiny spheres. The cooled contents were poured out and the powdered charcoal was washed away. The globules were then sorted by size. To anchor them to the jewelry, an animal glue was used, to which a copper salt was added. The Etruscans knew that copper and gold in combination melt at lower temperatures than is normally required for each metal. When heat was applied, the copper in the fixative dissolved and produced an oxygen reduction, causing both the gold on the surface of the beads and the backing to melt simultaneously and adhere to the copper. Granules thus applied served not only to produce glittering ornaments, but also to cover up seams, holes, and soldering spots.

In the enlargement above, gold granules cling to the wings of tiny ducks to form part of the lively surface of the 12-inch-long, seventh-century-BC fibula seen at left. The pin—which includes five lions as well as 55 ducks— is covered with 120,000 gold granules. It formed part of the treasure found in 1836 in the richly appointed Regolini-Galassi Tomb at Cerveteri.

like these were working in Etruscan cities early in the seventh century. Among the evidence is a mixing bowl, found at Caere, decorated and signed by a Greek vase painter named Aristonothos, suggesting that he may have lived there before 650 BC.

The Italian archaeologist Mario Torelli unearthed additional proof of the Greek presence while excavating in 1969 at Porto Clementino, near the mouth of the Marta River about 50 miles northwest of Rome. Torelli was primarily interested in probing the remains of Graviscae, a Roman port that had silted up long ago, but as he dug deeper, he discovered vestiges of an earlier harbor and realized that the first ships to use the harbor sailed not in Roman but in Etruscan times.

Historians have no way of knowing what the Etruscans called the harbor but assume that it was one of at least three serving the prosperous maritime city of Tarquinia, located about five miles in-

The Etruscans traded over a wide expanse, as suggested by this map, which shows commercial routes radiating from the area of their economic influence to locations as far south as Carthage, in present-day Tunisia, as far north as Hassle, Sweden, and as far west as Huelva, Spain. Archaeologists have also found remains of Etruscan pottery at such sites as the eastern shores of the Aegean and Mediterranean Seas and the banks of the Nile, but they cannot say for sure what route— or people—conveyed the pieces there.

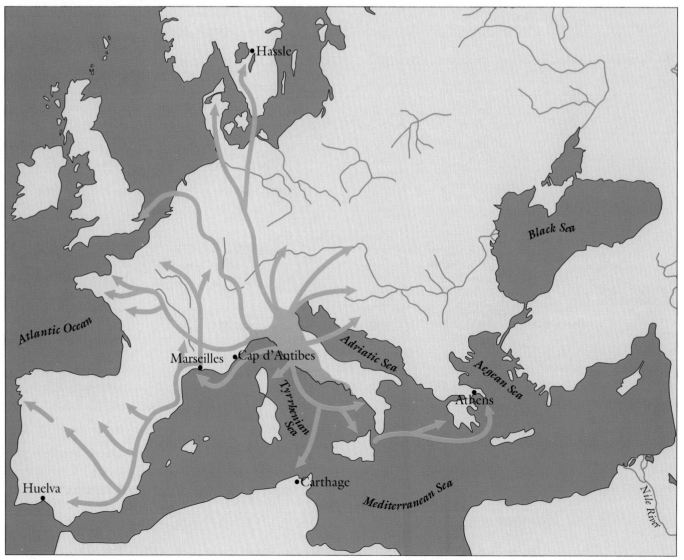

land. Torelli's findings—which included two wells and numerous postholes for wattle-and-daub huts—indicated that the port had been active as early as the seventh century BC and, more important, that it had housed a community of Greek merchants.

Though these foreigners were permitted to live on Etruscan soil, they were not integrated into the local population. Rather, they formed a self-contained community that the Tarquinians evidently took pains to keep at arm's length. Among its ruins Torelli discovered the remains of a small temple and a sanctuary dedicated to the Greek goddesses Hera, Demeter, and Aphrodite, as well as more than 5,000 votive oil lamps—an important element in Demeter's cult—most of them blackened from long years of use.

The excavators also uncovered an inscribed votive stone anchor about 4½ feet high that had apparently formed part of a funerary monument. The marker bore a representation of the god Apollo and a message in Greek, "I belong to Apollo of Aegina. Sostratos had me made." Scholars were quick to point out that the historian Herodotus wrote about a merchant from the Greek island of Aegina whose name was Sostratos. One of the most successful traders of his day, he reportedly possessed interests stretching as far afield as Spain.

To judge from the Regolini-Galassi Tomb and others like it, the most attractive commodity merchants such as Sostratos had to offer was Middle Eastern gold, channeled through the Euboean port of Al Mina on the Syrian coast. Yet in the long run the new knowledge and techniques the Greeks brought with them had a far more profound effect on Etruscan society—and especially on the arts, from architecture to metalwork and sculpture. Greek styles were widely adopted from the later decades of the seventh century BC on, when figures from Greek myth and epic poetry appeared with increasing frequency even in locally made products. The result was a startling upsurge in Etruscan creativity that brought about something of a golden age.

By far the most numerous Greek artifacts found on Etruscan soil are vases. A large number of them have come from a single site:

Birds, lotus buds, dancing figures, and geometric shapes adorn this 6½-inch-tall ostrich egg illegally taken from a seventh-century-BC Etruscan tomb. Highly prized by wealthy Etruscans, the eggs originated in central Africa and were often painted by Phoenician and Syrian artisans before being carried by traders to Etruria. There, as symbols of life, they were often entombed with the dead. The fashion for them lasted only from 700 to 600 BC.

the cemetery of Vulci, which in the early 19th century sat on land owned by the prince of Canino, Lucien Bonaparte—the brother of the French emperor. A peasant discovered the necropolis in 1828, when the ground collapsed beneath his plow. Pressed for cash, the prince immediately began to excavate and to sell. Within four months, his workers had unearthed more than 2,000 artifacts, the great majority of them vases, and the flow continued unabated for many years. The excavators apparently revealed a large number of non-Greek pots as well, but they paid little attention to them, since most were small or damaged and therefore deemed lacking in commercial value. According to George Dennis, the workers destroyed every bit of black clay they came across. This, of course, was the Etruscans' own lustrous bucchero, which scholars believe they developed in the first half of the seventh century BC as a less costly substitute for objects made of bronze (page 48-49).

The sheer number of Greek vases found at Vulci and other Etruscan tombs in the 18th and early 19th centuries was so great that it had a deflationary effect on the prices collectors were willing to pay for them. One observer writing in 1839 noted that their value had been so reduced that a vase "for which the King of Naples, not many years ago, gave ten thousand crowns, would now hardly be valued at more than two thousand." But on the whole, such vessels remained highly prized, and costly, items.

The profusion of Greek-style pottery inevitably raised the question of whether all the vases came from Greece, and the answer seems to be no. The earliest vases recovered in Etruria are distinguished by meander and zigzag patterns arranged in horizontal bands. As time went on, conventionally drawn figure scenes were sometimes added. Vases such as these were imported from Greece, but some were produced in the Greek colonies in Italy. Etruscan artisans also began to manufacture pottery in the Greek manner to please local tastes. The majority of the Vulci finds belong to an even later phase influenced by Corinthian pottery, which features representational designs and floral and arabesque patterns inspired by Middle Eastern motifs. Such vessels were also common in Caere, which, like Vulci, had a local school of potters.

From the late seventh century BC on, a new fashion for pottery from Athens, by then a rising star in the Greek political firmament, overtook the Corinthian mode. This ware initially featured black, glossy figures silhouetted against a background of Athens's

OBJECT OF A VENGEFUL GUARD'S FURY

One of the greatest of Greek treasures (below, right), the sixth-century-BC François Vase, or krater, has had a bizarre history since 1844, when it was discovered in fragments in the remains of two Etruscan tumuli. Purchased by Tuscany's grand duke Leopold II for the Uffizi, the piece was reassembled from the surviving sherds, some of which were missing, and put on display. It remained safe in a glass case until 1900 when a mentally disturbed guard, angry at his supervisor, smashed the tall ceremonial vessel into 638 pieces.

Would-be restorers from all over Italy applied to have the honor of trying to reconstruct the krater. At first it seemed that this unique portrayal of Greek legends, with all the characters named in more than 100 inscriptions, would be lost forever. But through a patient two-year effort the vessel was reassembled, with a fragment that meanwhile had turned up at the excavation site reinserted. Lacking, however, was a piece that a visitor to the museum had pocketed "as a souvenir" at the time of the vase's destruction. An appeal was made for its return and finally this too was presented to the museum, but too late for inclusion.

In 1973 a third restoration was undertaken when inspection of the vase after cleaning revealed that the surface was afflicted by microfractures. These had been produced over the years by sharp seasonal variations in temperature—the vase had been exhibited near a window—and by vibrations caused by visitors' footsteps and traffic outside. A study showed that within three years the vessel would have shattered. For this restoration the krater had to be taken apart (allowing for the inclusion of the tourist's memento) and rebuilt with modern techniques and soluble adhesives. It is now shown in a specially designed glass case equipped with suspension to protect the vase from even the slightest movement.

characteristic pinkish red clay, but after 525 BC the figures appeared in the natural color of the clay against a blacked-in background. Some of the black-figured vases were specifically designed for the Etruscan market and exported to Etruria, where they proved immensely popular. The later, red-figured vessels also found their way to the Etruscan cities in the fifth century BC, but in smaller amounts than the earlier pots, and they were less influential on the local potters.

Probably the most famous Attic black-figure piece to be found in Etruria was a large krater, or mixing bowl, known by the name of its discoverer—the Italian archaeologist Alessandro François. A widely traveled young scholar, François had already excavated at Cortona and at Cosa, a third-century-BC Roman coastal settlement near Vulci, before he came across pieces of the vessel near Chiusi in 1844.

Though the vase turned out to be only two-thirds complete when the fragments were examined, its great significance was obvious immediately: More than two feet tall and dating to 570 BC, the krater was adorned with six friezelike bands containing in excess of 200 figures from Greek mythology. Some are portrayed celebrating the wedding of Thetis, the mother of the Trojan War hero Achilles. Inscriptions in Greek identified not only the immortals, including Zeus and his wife Hera, but also the potter who made the vase, Ergotimos, and its painter, Kleitias.

The krater's beauty stirred passionate feelings among the antiquarians of the day. In fact, one of them persuaded François to return to Chiusi the following year in search of missing pieces. The archaeologist found five large sherds—enough for the vase to be restored and sold to the grand duke of Tuscany, but not enough for the bowl to be put together completely.

Although Greek influence on Etruscan cultural life was pervasive, the two societies remained very different. Etruscans had their own style of dress and religion and spoke an entirely separate language. The two cultures' customs and social structures were at odds with one another in many respects, from the position of women to attitudes toward democracy. Even in the arts, the Etruscan contribution remained distinctive; however much they may have learned from the Greeks in the heady days following the initial contact, Etruscan artists continued to reveal an unclassical enthusiasm for the spontaneous and the commonplace, the violent and the grotesque.

Much that the Etruscans did take from the Greeks they subsequently passed on to their neighbors in Italy and the peoples of northern Europe. One example of this cultural transmission, ripe with significance for the future, was the cultivation of the vine and wine making. Not only did the Etruscans themselves plant the first vineyards in the Chianti and Orvieto districts of Tuscany, which are still centers of the Italian wine trade today, but they also shared their knowledge with their northern trading partners, the Gauls. Divers swimming off Cap d'Antibes on the French Riviera confirmed this in 1955, when they turned up an ancient shipwreck carrying a cargo of Etruscan wine vessels estimated to date from 575-550 BC. Archaeologists have also found consignments of intact amphorae on the banks of the Rhône and Saône Rivers and a bronze Etruscan wine jug and basins in Côte-d'Or, Burgundy. On the strength of such evidence, historians claim that it was the Etruscans who originally carried the taste for wine to France.

However close the cultural links between the Greeks and the Etruscans may have been, rival political and commercial ambitions caused tension between the two factions and eventually led to open conflict. First, around the year 580 BC, Greeks and Etruscans from Caere fought a naval battle near the Aeolian Islands north of Sicily for control of the Strait of Messina. Then, in the mid sixth century, the Greeks colonized Corsica, thereby directly challenging Etruscan hegemony in the Tyrrhenian Sea and sparking a second confrontation around the year 535 BC. Although the Greek ships had the better of the fighting, the colonists were sufficiently weakened to be forced to quit the island.

According to Herodotus, the Etruscans stoned the Greek prisoners taken in the struggle—an act of impiety for which the inhabitants of Caere were supposedly visited with an epidemic, a form of divine retribution. Yet so close were the cultural ties linking the two peoples that the Etruscans looked to Greece for a cure. Caere's

The seated men and women in this terracotta plaque from Murlo, dating to about 575 BC, may be gods and goddesses or a high-ranking noble with his wife and entourage. Their exalted status is indicated by the folding stools and throne, symbols of power and importance in Etruria. Other signs of status are the situla, or bucket; fan; two-edged battle ax; and large staff held by the servants dutifully standing by.

A stylized portrait of the deceased graces the top of a sixth-century urn from Chiusi (ancient Clusium) containing his ashes. Crafted of terra cotta or bronze, these jars were often seated on thrones, lending an air of importance and dignity to the memory of the dead.

citizens sent envoys to the famous oracle of Apollo at Delphi to find out how to atone for their wrong. They were told that communal health and harmony would be restored if games were organized for the murdered prisoners on the Greek model. Apparently satisfied with the efficacy of the remedy, the city thenceforth maintained a treasury at the sacred site, even though it lay more than 600 miles away across the Adriatic Sea.

Classical authors offer revealing insights into Etruscan internal affairs in the wake of the momentous encounter with Greek civilization. They indicate that the cities were ruled by officials called lucumones, whose power may have developed when groups of villages first came together into city-states in the eighth century BC. Exactly what the lucumo's functions were remains unclear. A Roman source refers to the lucumo as a priest rather than as a king, suggesting that the duties of the post may later have been primarily religious. Historians surmise that real power in each city-state may have been exercised by an oligarchy made up of the leading families, who certainly controlled much of the available wealth.

There was also, however, a tradition of more personal and charismatic leadership, and its best-known exemplar was Lars Porsenna, who ruled Clusium—modern Chiusi—in the late sixth century BC. A favorite among 19th-century English schoolchildren, who learned about him through one of the most popular ballads in Thomas Babington Macaulay's 1842 collection, *Lays of Ancient Rome*, Porsenna evidently laid siege to Rome toward the end of the Tarquin dynasty: "Lars Porsenna of Clusium / By the Nine Gods he swore / That the great house of Tarquin / Should suffer wrong no more."

The poem went on to describe how, in the face of the Etruscan onslaught, a determined Roman warrior named Horatius single-handedly defended a wooden bridge that spanned the Tiber while his comrades struggled to cut it down, thereby forbidding the invaders access to the city. When the structure finally collapsed beneath him, the hero leaped into the river fully armed, but "borne up bravely by the brave heart within," he swam back to the Roman shore.

Macaulay, an English politician, historian, and pundit, took the story from the patriotic Roman historian Livy, who recounted that Lars Porsenna was so impressed by the Romans' courage that he eventually gave up and went home. Flattering though this version may have been to Roman sensibilities, it unfortunately seems to be untrue. Later Roman writers, including Tacitus and Pliny the Elder, record that Lars Porsenna took the city, and modern scholars support their view. The lucumo's troops apparently overran not just Rome itself but all of the surrounding countryside as well, triggering a conflict with the Greeks of southern Italy.

The incursion took place after Tarquinius Superbus, the last Etruscan king of Rome, was expelled from the city, and it may be that, far from seeking to defend the honor of the Tarquins, Porsenna was in fact trying to fill the power vacuum left by their overthrow. In any event, the adventure was short-lived: A combined force of Romans and Greeks defeated and killed Porsenna's son in 506 BC, ending the Etruscan hold on Rome once and for all.

Livy casts an interesting sidelight on the comportment of Etruscan rulers as a whole in another anecdote about Lars Porsenna. According to the historian, Porsenna was the target of an assassination attempt during the siege of Rome. His attacker managed to penetrate the Etruscan camp and found the leader seated beside his secretary while the soldiers were being paid. But the two men were dressed so similarly that the killer chose the wrong target and stabbed

An outcropping of rocks and overgrown vegetation camouflage tombs cut into the cliffs at Castel d'Asso, the site of an Etruscan settlement 50 miles north of Rome. Painted by British artist and draftsman Samuel James Ainsley in 1842, the watercolor captures the romantic quality of the Tuscan countryside that so delighted 19th-century European travelers. Ainsley, who accompanied George Dennis on his early excursions, contributed drawings to Dennis's The Cities and Cemeteries of Etruria.

the secretary rather than the king. If the story can be believed—and if the Clusian leader was in any way typical of other lucumones—it would suggest that the Etruscan elite did not reserve the trappings of majesty all to themselves, since even a lowly assistant dressed as elegantly as a mighty ruler.

Each lucumo exercised control only in his own territory, for the city-states remained totally autonomous. Though some scholars theorize that meetings of some kind took place at a site near Siena known as Poggio Civitate *(pages 71-81)*, Livy wrote that the event that regularly brought the 12 city-states together was an annual festival held at the sanctuary of Voltumna, an important national god. The site, ancient Volsinii, has not been located exactly, though it is known to have stood in the neighborhood of Orvieto, 65 miles north of Rome. The gathering provided an opportunity for matters of common concern to be discussed, and the lucumones apparently chose one of their number as their titular head for the coming year, but the post seems to have had no political power.

Given the lack of any central authority, the territorial expansion that occurred from about 700 BC on must have been the work of individual city-states or isolated groups of people. In the south, the city of Capua, about 20 miles north of modern Naples and dangerously close to the Greek colony of Cumae, became the nucleus of the Etruscan presence. Although relations were initially peaceful, they deteriorated in the course of the sixth century, to the Etruscans' cost.

To the north, settlers apparently started crossing the Apennines in large numbers sometime after 600 BC, establishing another important center of Etruscan culture at Bologna, then called Felsina, about 60 miles beyond the borders of Etruria proper. From there, Etruscan influence spread out along the Po Valley to the Adriatic, where the port of Spina became a major commercial center. These northern and eastern outposts were to play an important role in forging commercial and cultural links with Europe beyond the Alps.

Regardless of when these new urban centers sprang up, a common, unifying feature soon marked the landscape that surrounded them—cities of the dead, or necropolises, often made up of mounds covering burials. These tumuli are frequently the only accessible remains of the once-bustling metropolises. And so it has been primarily the tombs that have served as the point of contact for generations of travelers and archaeologists eager to learn about the Etruscans. The richness of the goods the graves contained, the beauty of the art that adorned them, and their often remarkable placement—whether near Spina in the Po Delta or on the plain surrounding Capua—have made Etruria as popular among modern researchers as it was among educated travelers of the 18th and 19th centuries, especially the English.

One of the first wandering scholars was James Byres, a Scottish architect and antiquary who spent much of his life guiding foreign visitors around the classical sites of Rome. Though his most ambitious project, a manuscript begun in 1766 entitled *History of the Etruscans and Their Antiquities*, sadly vanished, drawings made for it remain. Published years after his death, they provide an invaluable visual record of tomb interiors that otherwise would have been lost to the ages.

A charming English gentlewoman and antiquarian by the name of Lady Caroline Hamilton Gray, the author of the popular account *Tour to the Sepulchres of Etruria in 1839*, followed in Byres's footsteps in the 19th century. She arrived in Etruria via the English Midlands, where she lived in a drafty old castle, after doctors counseled her to winter in Italy—advice she and her husband, a curate, followed with such vigor that they ended up spending almost as much time traveling as performing parochial duties.

Intellectually active and accustomed to moving in the same circles as Macaulay, Dickens, and Thackeray, the couple found Etruria to be ideal territory for indulging their love of travel and learning. Hamilton Gray reported that friends warned her of the difficulties she faced "on account of the wildness of the country and the want of accommodation on the road." Yet she met with little worse than discomfort on her travels, though in such cases she proved adaptable, noting once that "we found the yolk of an egg an excellent substitute for milk with our tea."

Hamilton Gray was fortunate in making her tour when she did, shortly after the burst of discoveries that followed on the ending of the Napoleonic Wars; much of what she had to report was new. Even so, she found that many of the recently found sites were deteriorating. A number of Tarquinia's celebrated wall paintings, for example, were already barely visible, despite the fact that they had been brought to light only a dozen years before.

The image of sedateness, Lady Caroline Hamilton Gray hardly looks the type to root about in Etruscan tombs. Her interest began in London in 1837 when she visited a collection of Etruscan artifacts at the British Museum. Later that year she accompanied her husband to Rome, where antiques shops filled with Etruscan items further whetted her desire to see the sites from which they came. Out of her experiences came her 1841 best-selling book, Tour to the Sepulchres of Etruria in 1839.

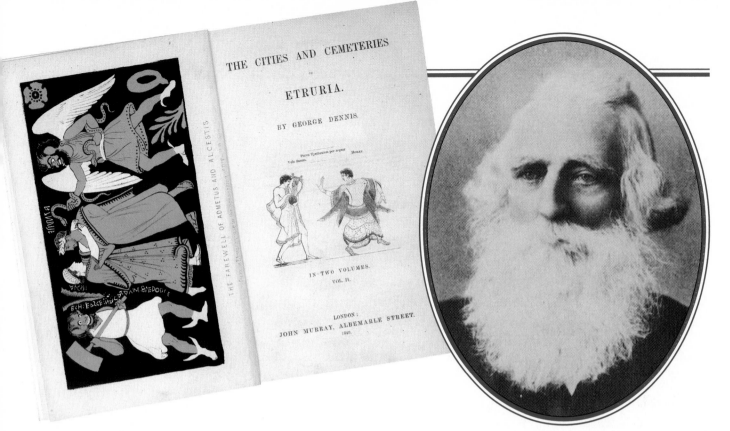

George Dennis is pictured above, right, 30 years after the first edition of his book, The Cities and Cemeteries of Etruria, *was issued in 1848. Published in two volumes, the richly illustrated work had an astonishing 1,085 pages, a number made even more impressive since Dennis was only 34 when it appeared. In 1878 a new, revised edition was issued, which, according to Dennis's biographer Dennis Rhodes, "was the climax of his wonderful achievement on the life and death of the Etruscan people."*

Tarquinia, however, was still a source of many surprises, including sarcophagus lids sculpted to resemble their owners. Before entering one tomb, Hamilton Gray later commented, "I was so much startled as to shrink back; for, the moment the door was opened, the stern, dignified, and colossal visage of an Etruscan chief stared me in the face. He looked as if he had just raised his head from the placid, majestic repose in which he lay, like the guardian of the sepulchre, and I could almost fancy he frowned on us as unwelcome intruders on his last resting-place."

Though Hamilton Gray often perceived little more than faded paint, rubble, and dust when she visited a necropolis, in her mind's eye she caught glimpses of towers and tunnels, sphinxes, chimeras of alabaster and stone—and merrymaking flesh-and-blood Etruscans. She cautioned tourists who did not possess "imagination sufficient to recall and reanimate the dust from the sepulchre" to expect disappointment.

"One man," she wrote, "goes to visit the relics of antiquity as he would to see some new invention or freshly discovered wild animal, of the nature of which no previous knowledge could be acquired. Another is as familiar with the ancient modes of thinking and acting as with the people whose house was burnt down yesterday, and the whole arrangement of which is easily traced through its ruins. The one converses with antiquity, and returns delighted and instructed from his visit; the other stares at it, and learns nothing."

Hamilton Gray's book, which did much to popularize Etruscan studies in its day, served as a trailblazer for George Dennis's more ambitious work, *The Cities and Cemeteries of Etruria*, which came out in England seven years later. Indeed, Dennis confidentially wrote to his publisher that *Tour to the Sepulchres* was one reason why he sought early publication of his classic. "Mrs. Gray has brought forth, I hear, a fourth edition," Dennis wrote, "and I would fain put a full stop to her erroneous progeny."

The appeal of Dennis's book rested on a combination of conscientious research and meticulous observation, brought to life by a literary gift every bit as vivid as Hamilton Gray's. While scholars appreciated the detailed record of individual sites, many of which could be reached only with great difficulty at the time, general readers enjoyed it for the author's emotional response to the picturesque and romantic landscapes in which they lay.

The contrast between such inspired impressionism and the technological bent of modern Etruscan fieldwork could hardly be more marked. Archaeological research today is increasingly a group activity, and it has access to techniques that the 19th-century pioneers could never have dreamed of.

Many of the methods were devised as responses to the ever more ruinous threat that modern civilization poses to the old. Deep plowing, for instance, sometimes with the aid of bulldozers, has done considerable harm, while fertilizers—used until the tombs were declared state property—raised the salt concentration of the water that continually seeps into them, damaging wall paintings as the salt leaches out and crystallizes on and behind their surfaces.

Confronted with the challenge of locating and investigating hidden Etruscan remains before they are irretrievably damaged, Etruscologists turned to aerial photography, which enabled them to take in entire sites at a glance. Italian army engineers were providing archaeologists with views taken from balloons as long ago as the years before World War I. But the technique was not applied systematically until 1944, when John Bradford, an English intelligence officer, noticed something in the reconnaissance photographs he examined during World War II.

Bradford realized that the images showed telltale signs of ancient human activity that were effectively invisible at ground level. Patches of grass that appeared lighter in color than the surrounding vegetation, for instance, indicated the presence of stony rubble—and

A restorer cleans the surface of a stone grave marker, called a cippus, discovered in 1986 near the vanished Etruscan city of Tuscania. Funerary steles such as this, carved to look like a house, are found in front of tombs throughout the Tuscan countryside. Others are pyramidal, circular, or cubical in shape. Many bear the names of the families buried there.

A shrine tomb of the sixth or fifth century BC stands in a necropolis outside the ruins of Populonia. Known as the Tomb of the Bronze Statuette, it was plundered in antiquity and named for the single funerary offering that remained behind. Populonia, the only major Etruscan city located on the coast, was the site of a large ironworking center. As a result, many of its tombs, including this one, wound up hidden under heaps of iron slag.

therefore the remains of flattened tumuli—in the underlying soil. Islands of gray soil surrounded by Tuscany's typical orange-brown dirt, the result of centuries of plowing, revealed the same thing. And shadows cast by slanting morning or evening light often threw into relief time-worn earthworks that Bradford called "shadow sites."

Analyzing these and other subtle clues, he succeeded in identifying nearly 2,000 previously unnoticed burial mounds in southern Etruria, thereby sparing them from further ravages of the farmer's plow. Bradford also produced the first accurate plans of the cemeteries, showing the roads and paths that once intersected them, and later applied the technique to regions as far apart as Roman England and classical Rhodes.

Bradford readily admitted that there were limitations to what aerial photography could achieve. Because remains must lie close to the surface in order to show up in such pictures, it has been estimated that only about half the tombs in the cemetery at Cerveteri and a quarter of those at Tarquinia were revealed from the air. Moreover, pinpointing the earthly location of sites discovered from on high has never been easy.

The sheer number of the tumuli also caused problems, for the excavation of even one to accepted archaeological standards was, and is, a costly and time-consuming business. And as the great majority

of tombs investigated turned out to be empty, looted by tomb robbers either in antiquity, during the Middle Ages, or recently, the results rarely justified the labor and expense.

Fortunately, an Italian engineer named Carlo Lerici devised a way to investigate unopened tombs that avoided the need for lengthy digging. After retiring from a successful business career, Lerici devoted much of the money he had made to establishing a foundation that at first had little to do with Etruria. Rather, it was intended to devise new ways of finding subterranean supplies of oil, water, gas, or ores. But when relatives asked Lerici to design a family mausoleum, he looked to ancient architecture for inspiration, and soon his thoughts turned to the Etruscans. Then he learned of Bradford's work.

"I am an engineer, not a trained archaeologist," he wrote. "But for some years now I have been fascinated both by the mysteries of the Etruscans and by the challenges of using modern geophysical techniques to hunt for buried clues to the past. One such technique is aerial photography."

Using pictures taken from the air to find tombs to investigate, Lerici then established their exact location by painstakingly plotting variations in the soil's ability to conduct electricity. Metal rods were planted in the ground and a current was passed between them so that the resistance could be assessed. Then the rods were moved repeatedly and new measurements taken. The presence of a tomb was normally marked by an elevated reading, since air offers more resistance than earth to the passage of electricity.

Investigating tombs spotted in wartime reconnaissance photographs, Carlo Lerici, kneeling, developed a technique for peering inside them without actually opening them. Here, he scrutinizes readings on instruments measuring underground electrical currents, which enables him to pinpoint one of the burials before inserting a camera through a hole bored in the ceiling. In the shot of the tomb below, a flash illuminates the chamber so that archaeologists can determine whether to excavate it or not.

Taken in 1944 by the British Royal Air Force during a drought, this photograph of the Banditaccia cemetery reveals hundreds of circular tumuli invisible from the ground. John Bradford, an RAF officer stationed in Italy during World War II, noticed such "ghost" tombs as he examined reconnaissance shots.

Once the exact center of the tomb had been established, Lerici used an electric drill to bore a test hole deep enough to pierce the chamber's ceiling, usually about 15 to 20 feet. He then lowered in a specially built periscope that enabled him to view the interior. If it contained items of interest, he took pictures with a military spy camera the size of a cigarette lighter mounted in the end of a long, watertight, aluminum tube that also contained a tiny flash apparatus. By revolving the device 30 degrees between shots, a complete panorama of the interior of the sepulcher could be obtained in just a dozen photographs. The probe was then withdrawn, and the hole closed up quickly to minimize the risk of air damage to the tomb. Sites shown to be worth investigating further could then be excavated in the traditional manner.

The Lerici probe was to prove spectacularly successful. Within 10 years of its development it had been used to explore almost 1,000 burial chambers at Cerveteri and more than 5,000 at Tarquinia, where several painted tombs were located—as many, Lerici claimed, as had been found in the entire 19th century. Among them was the so-called Tomb of the Olympiad, illustrated with scenes of running, boxing, chariot racing, and other sports. The first important painted sepulcher to be opened in 67 years, it was discovered prior to the Rome Olympic Games of 1960, which influenced its name.

Despite the innovative technology, Lerici's work continued to be hampered by an age-old problem—tomb robbers. Aware of his methods and past successes, they watched his every move and on at least one memorable occasion at Cerveteri in 1958 beat the engineer to a tomb that he had found to contain valuable antiquities. King Gustav VI Adolf of Sweden—himself an enthusiastic amateur archaeologist *(pages 102-103)*—had been invited to open the chamber, one of a series that Lerici had previously photographed. But thieves struck on the eve of the royal visit. Forced to move fast in order to avoid embarrassment, Lerici's colleagues substituted another tomb for the king to uncover.

What the king finally exposed—pottery, some jewelry, a funeral bed hewn from rock—was not momentous in import. But even small finds count when it comes to the Etruscan past, if only because these discoveries can supply further insights into the kind of people the Etruscans were. Deprived of their language by time, they must speak to the modern world through their artifacts. And in these they live once more.

In 1965 Pennsylvania's Bryn Mawr College agreed to sponsor an excavation in Tuscany, to be led by archaeologist Kyle Meredith Phillips Jr. The purpose was to find a site that could be used as a training ground for archaeology students. Phillips finally settled on a place called Poggio Civitate (Inhabited Hill), an isolated hilltop near the village of Murlo, southeast of Siena.

Excavations began in the summer of 1966; since then, teams sponsored by various colleges and composed of professionals and students have descended on Poggio Civitate yearly. The project has turned out to be far more than a teaching tool. It has also produced discoveries unprecedented in the study of the Etruscan civilization—which had previously been known largely from examination of its sanctuaries and cemeteries.

Perhaps the most significant find was the remains of a monumental building some 200 feet square. Located on the topmost excavated layer of the site, the edifice was topped by a number of life-size, seated terra-cotta figures, one of them waggishly dubbed the Cowboy because of its broad-brimmed headgear *(above)*. Referred to as the Upper Building, this structure probably stood between 600 and 530 BC. Beneath its foundations lay remains of an earlier structure, known as the Lower Building; constructed in the seventh century BC, this one seems to have been destroyed by accidental fire toward the end of the century. Nearby are the ruins of a large workshop.

Artifacts from the site have been exhibited around the world and are now on display at a special museum in Murlo. A selection of them is shown on the following pages, against the backdrop of a decorative terra-cotta frieze from the Upper Building.

A SURPRISE AT POGGIO CIVITATE

After scouting through the tangled vegetation that overlay Poggio Civitate, Kyle Phillips and his band of archaeology students decided to sink their first exploratory trenches in a section of the hill that locals called Piano del Tesoro, or Plateau of the Treasure. There, students had come across a fragment of an ancient clay storage jar protruding from the ground and surmised that other artifacts would probably be found below. Indeed, Phillips would write later, "within hours we knew that we were excavating human occupation."

Strangely, though, most of what the diggers found was shattered: Pottery, statuary, decorative terra-cotta friezes—nearly everything seemed to have been delib-

large Upper Building that emerged over several seasons of digging. Given its size and elaborate decoration, the structure must have held a preeminent position in the community, but what its exact function was continues to elude scholars.

By the mid 1980s, successive teams of students had come to Poggio Civitate, completed excavation of the Upper Building, and unearthed traces of the Lower Building and the Workshop, as seen at right.

Overgrown with scrub trees and thick underbrush, the gentle contours of Poggio Civitate loom over an expanse of carefully tended Tuscan farm fields in a photograph (above) *taken in the summer*

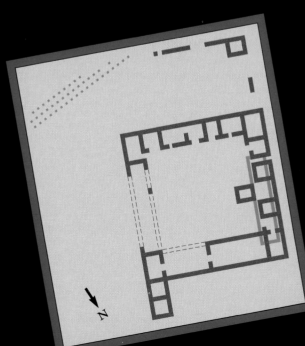

The rough stone foundations of the
Upper Building lie exposed in this 1972 photo-
graph (top). In the inset, the battered terra-cotta face of the
seated figure with broad-brimmed hat is seen as it was found
amid the structure's ruins.

In this ground plan of the three structures identified thus far at
Poggio Civitate, dark blue indicates the Upper Building, green
the Lower Building, and red the Workshop. The narrow, blue
dotted lines mark portions of the Upper Building where the
foundation has yet to be excavated.

MYSTERY OF THE UPPER BUILDING

Several years into the excavations at Poggio Civitate, Kyle Phillips became steadfastly convinced that the Upper Building had not been a temple, as he had first supposed. Noting its large courtyard and surrounding rooms, he concluded that the building was the central meeting hall of a league of Etruscan cities. It had been ritually demolished, he theorized, by an ascendant rival power.

Some scholars disagree with this interpretation, however, still holding that the building was a temple or a sanctuary, or even the palatial home of a rich Etruscan.

Whatever its function may have been, the perplexing structure was richly festooned with decorative terracotta figures, among them the pair shown above. And the roof was crowned with numerous statues, several wearing their distinctive broad-brimmed hats.

The Upper Building's ample central courtyard is clearly visible in this reconstructed view, which also shows the expansive, tile-covered pitched roofs that topped the structure.

A digger brushes dirt from one of several frieze plaques found lying near a corner of the Upper Building. The friezes feature horse races, banquets, processions, and assemblies of gods or dignitaries.

This terra-cotta sphinx decorated the building's roofline along with seated figures wearing broad-brimmed hats and perhaps 25 other human and animal figures. The meaning of these statues remains a mystery.

BONE GRIFFIN

DELICATE TREASURES SAVED BY FIRE

Like the Upper Building that rose on its foundations, the Lower Building displayed on its roof many large geometric terra-cotta cutouts, as well as figures of animals and a horse and rider—fairly common ornaments among the early Etruscans *(opposite)*. But the structure's remains also yielded an undreamed-of trove of small, elegantly crafted items that spoke not only of the skill of Poggio Civitate's artisans, but also of the wealth of those who had once used the Lower Building.

Kyle Phillips, shown above as he examines some of the myriad decorative pieces unearthed at the site, noted that the finds "give precious insights into life in Northern Etruria during the seventh century BC." Among other things, they showed that trade goods

reaching the coast of the Tyrrhenian Sea found their way inland to smaller cities. Many of the artifacts in ivory, amber, and faience attest to commercial relations with North Africa, the Baltic, and the Levant.

Some scholars maintained that such exquisite workmanship was beyond the capabilities of provincial artisans. But discoveries in the ruins of the nearby Workshop have indicated that many of the delicate articles were probably crafted right at Poggio Civitate.

Less than an inch tall, the four items at top and right are among many such pieces from the ruins of the Lower Building. Some were discolored by the fire that destroyed the structure toward the end of the seventh century BC.

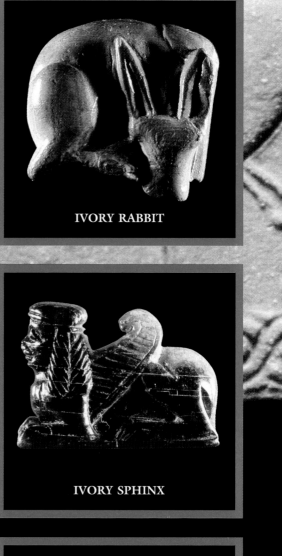

IVORY RABBIT

IVORY SPHINX

GEMSTONE ANIMAL GROUP

VARIED STATUES PLACED ON HIGH

Called acroteria, from the Greek for topmost place, terra-cotta representations of humans, animals, or various geometric figures were frequently used to ornament ridgepoles of Etruscan structures, as shown above in a reconstruction of Poggio Civitate's Lower Building. Although their exact purpose is unknown, they may have had symbolic meaning.

The earliest acroteria were probably nothing more than relatively simple wooden cutouts embellishing the roofs of huts. In time, these evolved into more expressive—but still two-dimensional—figures such as the terra-cotta horse and rider below, pieced together from the finds of several years. Later still, perhaps influenced by Greek sculpture, Etruscan artisans began fashioning more sophisticated three-dimensional images like the seated figures and the sphinx decorating the roof of the Upper Building.

DEBRIS OF AN ANCIENT WORKSHOP

In the summer of 1982 diggers at Poggio Civitate unearthed the foundations of the third major structure discovered so far. The project's codirector, Erik O. Nielsen of the University of Evansville in Indiana—who would succeed Kyle Phillips as head of the excavations when Phillips died in 1988—identified the ruins as the remnant of a once-thriving Workshop that produced many of the goods found at the site. The tile-roofed Workshop appeared to have had no walls; it was open on all four sides for light and ventilation.

The highly vitrified tiles and the concentration of carbon found in the debris indicated that the building had been destroyed by fire, probably in the same blaze that leveled the nearby Lower Building. And the fire had no doubt been sudden: In their haste to escape the flames, some of the artisans left behind footprints in still-wet clay tiles that lay drying on the workplace floor.

After brushing the dirt from footprints found in the Workshop's clay tiles (above), *conservators made plaster casts of the impressions. One such cast, clearly showing the form of an ancient artisan's bare foot, can be seen at left.*

Found associated with material contemporary with the Lower Building, the terra-cotta face shown above was one of many that decorated the structure's guttering system; to its right is a clay mold, discovered in the Workshop, that was used to mass-produce such faces. At right, a reconstructive drawing of the Workshop shows the building's open-walled design.

Evidence of the kind of objects that were produced in the Workshop is seen in these discards found in the dump to the north of the Lower Building. Digging over the years has yielded ivory, bone, and antler pieces in various stages of completion.

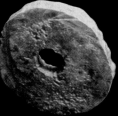

DOWN-TO-EARTH TRAINING

The yearly excavations at Poggio Civitate continue to yield major insights into Etruscan civilization. Sponsored by the University of Evansville and partially financed by students' tuition payments, the project also continues to yield rich benefits as an educational enterprise. Indeed, more than 50 participants in the program have gone on to attain professorships in archaeology or related areas.

The 15 to 20 American students who arrive at the site each summer for the eight-week session are given matchless training in the field. In addition to lectures on Etruscan culture and the ongoing discoveries at Poggio Civitate, they also receive hands-on experience in basic archaeological techniques—from digging and meticulous recordkeeping to the restoration and preservation of artifacts.

And there seems to be no end in sight. Project director Erik O. Nielsen—who first went to Murlo as a graduate student in 1970 and has returned every year since—has observed that in nearly three decades of digging only about 20 percent of the site has been excavated. At that rate, it seems, the exploration of Poggio Civitate could go on for generations to come.

In one of the workrooms at the excavation site, Erik Nielsen (above, right) shows one of his graduate students some of the fine points of Etruscan pottery. In the background are shelves of neatly boxed and cataloged artifacts from the site.

At top, a student makes meticulous ink drawings of the pieced-together fragments of a bucchero vessel unearthed at Poggio Civitate. In the inset, a student who has just uncovered a sherd of pottery records the find's precise size, condition, and location.

Working skillfully with a palette of watercolors and referring to a pair of terra-cotta heads that once decorated the guttering system of the Workshop, a Murlo summer student renders a life-size re-creation of the decorative gutter as it might have appeared during the building's heyday.

RHYTHMS AND DELIGHTS OF THE GOOD LIFE

As 19th-century lovers of antiquities painstakingly cleared away the dust of more than two millennia and opened the long-sealed tombs, the lost world of the Etruscans emerged once more into the daylight. On carved and painted surfaces, on the walls of the burial chambers, and upon the rich grave goods with which they were furnished, this vanished civilization left a record of its pleasures and preoccupations. In one tomb, hunters subdue lions with arrows, bows, and grim expressions. In another, dancers perform to clacking castanets and the pipe's persuasive wail. Here guests gossip at a banquet; there slaves scurry in a crowded kitchen. Elsewhere prisoners are sacrificed in a gory scene, or demons and winged horses, the denizens of Etruria's myths and dreams, march past on parade.

In 1850, while excavating a burial mound in a necropolis at Cerveteri, the site of ancient Caere, an Italian nobleman named Giampietro Campana exposed a staircase in the rock that led down to a most extraordinary tomb, guarded by two sculpted lions. Inside he found a painted chamber 21 feet long and 25 feet wide. A pair of square, seven-foot-high pillars seemingly supported the roof, and deep niches carved in the form of luxurious beds had been hollowed out of the stone forming the walls. Delighted by the rich array of shapes and colors, the curious carvings, and bold architectural detail,

A warrior in full battle gear pauses as a female companion proffers him a bowl, perhaps containing a libation. The figures form part of a fifth-century bronze candelabra from Marzabotto.

the marchese Campana christened his discovery *la tomba bella*—the beautiful tomb.

But as news of the discovery spread, Campana's find became widely known as the Tomb of the Reliefs, after its most spectacular feature *(pages 112-113)*. Virtually every surface—the walls of the chamber, the lintels and margins of the niches, the sides of the pillars—was adorned with meticulously crafted, realistic stucco models of animals, domestic furnishings, ritual objects, weapons, and the essential but often overlooked utensils of daily life. These ranged from a coiled rope to a perfume bottle to a pickax, from a leather handbag to a walking stick to a slightly mouse-nibbled wheel of cheese.

Many of the articles hung as if suspended from nails hammered into a kitchen or storeroom wall, ready to be lifted down and used in the routines of their ghostly owners. Neatly stacked within the central niche, sculpted pillows lay ready to receive a sleeper's head. At the bed's foot, a stucco chest held a folded linen book, also of stucco. Should the chamber's occupants awake and feel hungry, a competent cook would find everything necessary to prepare a meal: spoons and ladles, a knife rack holding two kinds of blade, spits for roasting meat, a pestle for pounding ingredients, a terra-cotta bowl adorned with bay leaves, a bronze jug full of imaginary wine.

Not every item was so easy to identify. Archaeologists, for instance, still argue over the purpose of a light yellow tray bearing 11 horizontal lines. Some scholars suggest that the ruled surface is a rudimentary counting device or a gaming board, while others hold that it was a wooden board for kneading and shaping pasta. And indeed, the tomb contains representations of two other tools, not unlike those found in the kitchens of modern cooks, that might have served a similar purpose—a wooden rolling pin for dough and a small toothed wheel of the sort used for cutting ravioli.

Etruscan inscriptions at the entrance to the chamber and within the niches identified the tomb's owners as a family called Matunas and named some of the persons whose remains rested there. The burial chamber had been built for one Vel Matunas and his wife Canatnei. Other occupants included their son Aule and daughter Ramtha and various male and female members of later generations. The weapons and other soldierly paraphernalia that decorated their resting place suggested that this was a clan with a proud military tradition. The obvious care and artistry that went into the creation of the sepulcher declared the family to be people of position who had

Painted soon after the discovery of the Tomb of the Reliefs in 1850, a watercolor by British artist Samuel James Ainsley depicts the near-pristine condition of the third-century-BC site. Littering the benches on which the dead were once laid out—and onto which a red pantalooned peasant can be seen climbing—are vases left behind by ancient mourners.

the resources to satisfy their sophisticated tastes. They had lived and died at the end of the fourth and beginning of the third century BC, by which time many Etruscans had been absorbed into the political sphere of Rome, but still retained their language, religion, and distinctive ethnic identity.

Because the Matunas family, in common with their fellow Etruscans of the upper classes, believed that they should enjoy an afterlife as pleasant, as beautiful, and as well ordered as the mortal existence that had gone before it—and because the artisans at their service displayed such a loving attention to detail—their tomb now provides a window into the sights, colors, textures, and even the likely sounds and smells of Etruscan daily life. By building themselves such a virtual home-away-from-home as this, they unwittingly let future generations peer upon their most intimate moments. And so it is with other Etruscan tombs whose owners still invite the curious to share their banquets, join their games and dances, admire the changing fashions within their wardrobes, and watch them—or, more accurately, their slaves and underlings—at work.

For centuries, the little that was known about the vibrant and sophisticated culture of the Etruscans came, of course, through the distorting glass of Greek and Roman writings. In the 19th century a clearer picture began to emerge, but it was far from complete—for an obvious reason: The homes and temples of the Etruscans, like many of their worldly goods, were constructed of perishable materials, so apart from the tombs, sites rich in Etruscan remains have been rare. Only with the application of advanced techniques in relatively recent times have archaeologists started finding evidence of settlement, agriculture, industry, and trade. As well as revealing the economic underpinnings of the graceful, seemingly leisured lives enjoyed by the Matunas family and their peers, these excavations are bringing forth clues about the era when the Etruscan revels came to an end.

As in every civilization, the poor have left little behind; most information about Etruscan lives comes from the memorials and relics of the rich. Yet there are slender traces, including some tomb paintings, of the slaves who served in affluent households. At least one family, by the name of Alfni, living near Clusium in the first century BC, commemorated its dead slaves by painting either their names or their duties in red letters upon the pots and urns that held their ashes. The maker of beds, the setter of tables, the man who dyed the family's cloth were all memorialized, as was a female retainer named Larthi who had married a man called Vel Percumsna.

Some slave names of this period suggest that the kitchens and domestic workshops of many wealthy homes must have been cosmopolitan environments, echoing with conversations, snatches of songs, and curses voiced in a rich amalgam of alien accents and tongues. Memorials survive to people whose names were obviously Etruscanized versions of foreign originals: among them, Greeks named Achilles, Evander, and Dionysos, a Judaean called Akiba, and an Egyptian whose name, Serapion, commemorated one of the ancient deities of his homeland on the Nile.

Apart from an observation by a Greek commentator that Etruscans flogged their slaves in time to the music of a pipe, little suggests that the lives of slaves in Etruria differed much from those led by their counterparts elsewhere, though some may have enjoyed relatively higher status. But where Etruscan society did stand in sharp contrast to its neighbors was in its treatment of women. Indeed, archaeological as well as documentary evidence reveals that Etruscan women enjoyed a degree of freedom and high social status unequaled anywhere else in the Mediterranean world.

Within the family tombs, women lay in resting places as handsomely appointed as those of their fathers, husbands, brothers, or sons. Many scholars, for instance, believe that the most prominent and imposing niche in the Tomb of the Reliefs was originally intended for a much-mourned daughter of the house of Matunas. And the possessions buried with a woman—ornate bronze mirrors, perfume flagons, vessels of precious metal—frequently bore her name. These grave goods also provide evidence to support the theory that Etruscan women, at least among the tomb-owning upper classes, were literate. The mirrors, found so far exclusively in women's burials, were richly decorated with mythological scenes incorporating engraved labels that identified the principal characters or—in one famous find from Volterra—explained the story.

Also within the tombs, memorial inscriptions reveal that upon marriage, women kept their first names and family surnames, unlike the matrons of Rome, whose identities were submerged within those of their husbands. No Etruscan woman would have put up with the meek wedding vows of a proper Roman wife, declaring that "as you are Gaius, I am Gaia."

Nor, like a good Greek wife, did Etruscan women closet themselves in their chambers. Wall paintings as early as the sixth cen-

The reverse sides of highly polished bronze Etruscan mirrors, such as the one at left, bear exquisitely engraved designs, usually on mythological themes. In the scene above, matrons attend a maiden, arranging her hair and headdress, perhaps on her wedding day. More than 3,000 of the mirrors survive to the present day, a major source of information about Etruscan customs and beliefs.

tury BC show them out and about, enjoying themselves on equal terms with men and mingling with them as spectators at sporting events. At banquets, they recline at ease on dining couches alongside male companions—unlike their latter-day Roman sisters who, if invited to join a party at all, would perch demurely on upright chairs.

These social arrangements did not go unnoticed among outside observers, whether they were Greek contemporaries or Romans looking backward. Coming from societies where women held few or no legal rights, lived and died according to the whim of father or husband, and—ideally—kept out of the public gaze, spinning and weaving in seclusion, these culture-shocked chroniclers may have misinterpreted, or willfully distorted, what they observed of Etruscan relationships between the sexes.

In the fourth century BC the Greek historian Theopompus titillated his readers with reports of Etruscan immorality, most of which he borrowed from earlier authors. Etruscan women, he announced, were perfectly happy to strip off their clothes in public and exercise alongside men in the gymnasium. At parties that in his view women had no business attending in the first place, they drank alcohol and proposed toasts as blatantly and publicly as any man. And both genders were equally guilty of loose conduct.

"There is no shame to be seen committing a sexual act in public," he gasped. "When they are at a gathering of friends, this is what they do: first of all, when they have finished drinking, and are ready for bed, and while the torches are still lighted, the servants bring in sometimes courtesans, sometimes handsome boys, sometimes their

A few years after the exquisite Tarquinia tombs came to light in 1830, artist-archaeologist Carlo Ruspi traced the paintings of the Triclinium (above) *and Querciola tombs* (right). *Scribbling color notes in the margins, he used his renderings to make color facsimiles. Often, these early tracings serve scholars as the truest record of Tarquinia's much disintegrated paintings today.*

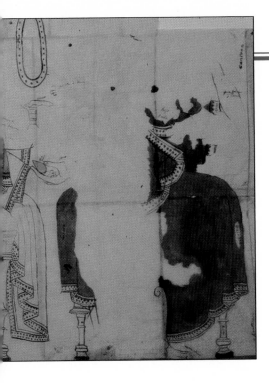

own wives. They all engage in making love, some watching one another, some isolating themselves with rattan screens set up round the couches, each couple wrapped in one cover."

Whether such tales were true or false, what seems to have shocked Theopompus most was the lack of furtiveness and hypocrisy. The images found in so many Etruscan tombs, of visibly affectionate husbands and wives embracing on their shared memorials, seemed alien in his sight. To be sure, vases show Greek men disporting themselves in an equally lusty fashion before the lights went out—but only with female courtesans and beautiful youths, not with their wives.

With such goings on, Theopompus declared, it was small wonder that the lovely ladies of Etruria were sometimes unable to identify the fathers of their newborns. And the children, he complained, grew up to be "like those who brought them up, and have many drinking parties, and they too make love with all the women."

Roman writers did little to correct such Greek notions, al-

though one of them, the historian Livy, credited certain formidable Etruscan women with playing crucial parts in Roman history back in the misty era when the young city was ruled by Etruscan kings. Indeed, in Livy's monumental history of Rome, compiled in the first century AD, a capable woman stood behind the first monarch, Lucius Tarquinius Priscus.

Livy uses the Etruscan word Lucumo to refer to the future king. Lucumo's wife was Tanaquil, a "woman of the most exalted birth." Though ambitious and wealthy, Lucumo was looked upon with disdain by his fellow Etruscans because his Greek father, Demaratus of Corinth, was an alien. "Not of a character lightly to endure a humbler rank in her new environment than she had enjoyed in the condition to which she had been born," as Livy put it, Tanaquil persuaded Lucumo to move from Tarquinia, their hometown, to Rome, which was more receptive to new settlers and was growing by leaps and bounds.

Packing their possessions into a covered wagon, the couple headed south. But before they could arrive, an eagle swooped out of the sky, snatched Lucumo's hat in its talons, and flew off. Then the bird descended and returned the headgear to its startled owner. The strange event filled Tanaquil with joy. Adept in the interpretation of omens, she told her spouse to expect "transcendent greatness."

Her prediction proved true—indeed, her husband soon attained the crown of Rome, thereby founding the Tarquin dynasty. He took the name Lucius Tarquinius Priscus, Lucius being the Latinized form of Lucumo. Tarquinius may have owed his achievement to the will of the Fates, expressed by the eagle, or to Tanaquil's own considerable skill at behind-the-scenes maneuverings. Whatever the case, she repeated her success: When the time came, she ensured that the omens were good and that the throne passed from her husband to her son-in-law Servius Tullius.

Nor was Tanaquil the last of her line to take matters into her own hands. Livy recounts the saga of Tanaquil's headstrong and restless granddaughter Tullia. She was the wife of a princely youth of gentle disposition. But her sister, who in Tullia's estimation "lacked a woman's daring," was married to the prince's violent brother, Lucius Tarquinius the Younger. Historians know him as Lucius Tarquinius Superbus. Concluding that her spouse lacked the gumption of his sibling, who hungered to be king, Tullia arranged for the murder of both her husband and her sister. With these obstacles disposed of, she allied herself with Tarquinius and encouraged him to take the throne from her own father, Servius Tullius.

"If you are he whom I thought I was marrying, I call you both man and king," Livy quoted Tullia as saying to her new husband, "if not, then I have so far changed for the worse, in that crime is added, in your case, to cowardice. Come, rouse yourself!"

Emboldened by such taunting, Tarquinius set to work trying to win political supporters by slandering the king. Then, in the company of armed henchmen, he burst into the senate and threw Servius out of the building. Half-fainting, the king was attempting to make his way to safety when assailants sent by Tarquinius mortally wounded him. Tullia raced to the senate to proclaim her husband the new king. Later, while riding home in her carriage, she came upon the body of her murdered father. Her driver was struck with terror and immediately pulled up on the reins, but Tullia—"crazed by the avenging spirits of her sister and former husband"—ordered him to gallop on, straight over the corpse. The daughter was showered in her father's blood in a gory scene. The site was known forever after as the Street of Crime.

In the hands of Livy, even the founding of the Roman republic was construed as a sexual morality tale, exposing the difference between Latin virtue and Etruscan decadence. In his version of history, a friendly competition between some Roman and Etruscan army officers caused the end of the rule of Rome by the Tarquins. To test the relative virtue of their wives, they made an unannounced visit to the Etruscan ladies and found them "at a luxurious banquet, whiling away the time with their young friends." A subsequent trip to the house of a Roman wife, Lucretia, revealed her sitting up late over her spinning, accompanied by her equally industrious maidens.

After the contest, one of the Etruscan officers, a member of the Tarquin family, vowed to rape Lucretia and returned to her house days later with sword in hand. Preferring death with honor to life in shame, Lucretia initially resisted her attacker, but when he threatened to disgrace her further by killing his slave and placing the naked body alongside hers as incriminating evidence of her faithlessness, her defenses were overcome. Later Lucretia tearfully denounced the violation to her male relations and asked them to punish the Etruscan. Then, saying that she acquitted herself of sin but could not absolve herself from punishment, she took a knife from beneath her dress and plunged it into her heart. To avenge her, the Romans went to war

ECHOES OF EVERYDAY LIFE AT A FORGOTTEN HILLTOP SETTLEMENT

Not all archaeological treasure consists of precious metal and jewels. Sometimes it can be as simple as cooking pots, clay spools, spindle whorls, loom weights, fire-blackened bricks, and countless potsherds, such as those Florida State University's Nancy Thomson de Grummond and her team have dug up at Cetamura del Chianti, one of the last Etruscan strongholds of the Hellenistic era. At a time when the southern Etruscan cities were disintegrating before Rome's social and political encroachment, small rural settlements like this one atop a high hill sprang up in the north and became home to ordinary citizens. Cetamura's inhabitants may even have been freedmen and slaves; there is no evidence of the presence of an elite class.

What makes such humble finds exciting is that they offer clues to lives of the common people. Although the Etruscans lived in settlements throughout Etruria, they are largely known by the lavish tombs and graves of the wealthy; relatively little attention has been given to actual habitation sites.

Even Cetamura's potsherds have information to reveal. Possibly utilized as scratch pads, they bear numbers, letters, and symbols that may have been employed in business transactions. Clay cups and bowls reveal two names, Lausini and Cluntni, perhaps those of their owners. In 1994, after four years of digging for the kiln where these vessels may have been fired, de Grummond (left, with site supervisor Charles Ewell) struck pay dirt. "Thousands of tombs have been found," she says, "but only some 20 Etruscan kilns. Cetamura's is sure to contribute novel information about this Etruscan industry."

Weaving implements, such as this clay loom weight with spindle whorls, shed light on the lives of Etruscan women, whether of lowly birth like the female inhabitants of Cetamura, or of royal status. Women's principal contribution to the economy lay in the spinning, weaving, and dyeing of cloth for the garments, hangings, and blankets needed by families and communities.

against the Tarquin house and drove the Etruscan kings from their territory. Soon Rome became a republic, and the virtuous Lucretia became a role model for Roman ladies.

If Greek observers, like the Romans, were displeased by the Etruscans' sexual mores, they were even less impressed by their dedication to the art of dining. The Greek philosopher and writer Posidonius clucked his disapproval or perhaps, well masked, his envy of "the fat Tyrrhenians": "Twice a day the Etruscans set a sumptuous table, with everything that contributes to a refined life; they make up the couches with embroidered coverlets, they set out a large quantity of silver vessels, and all is served by a considerable number of servants."

The testimony of the tomb paintings bears Posidonius out. Stepping into an excavated burial chamber at Tarquinia known as the Tomb of the Triclinium, the 19th-century English antiquarian George Dennis could almost hear the ripples of laughter and smell the food. "The first peep within this tomb is startling, especially if the sun's rays happen at the moment to enter the chamber," Dennis wrote. "Such a blaze of rich colour on the walls and roof, and such life in the figures that dance around! In truth, the excellent state of preservation—the wonderful brilliancy of the colours, almost as fresh after three or four and twenty centuries, as when first laid on—the richness of the costumes—the strangeness of the attitudes—the spirit, the vivacity, the joyousness of the whole scene—the decidedly Etruscan character of the design render this one of the most interesting tombs yet opened in Etruria."

Yet before these Etruscan gentlefolk could dine off the low three-legged tables set out before the triclinia, or couches, after which the tomb was named, hard work went on in the kitchen. In a tomb built at Orvieto in the late fourth century BC, a family named Leinie portrayed 11 servants preparing a funeral feast and duly supplied the workers with two-word inscriptions, apparently giving their names and positions within the kitchen brigade.

There would be plenty of meat for dinner: A slaughtered ox hangs upside down from a beam, with its head nearby, along with hare, venison, and assorted poultry. Wielding a hatchet, a boy chops up these raw ingredients. Behind him, the fire that will cook them is already well ablaze; it must be hot, for he wears nothing but an apron around his hips.

Another youth, also scantily clad in the kitchen's heat, plies two small, sturdy pestles, crushing and grinding some unseen blend of ingredients in a mortar, probably made of bronze, that is mounted on a tripod. Surviving ancient recipes suggest that well-pounded mixtures, spiked with pungent marinades and vigorously seasoned, appeared on the tables of rich and poor alike. The peasant might content himself with a simple paste of garlic, herbs, and wine, mixed with the same ewe's-milk cheese—pecorino—that more than 2,000 years later still remains a specialty of the region. The rich man, on the other hand, might have commanded his cook to concoct some savory amalgam of chicken breast, fennel, mint, date honey, mustard, oil, fermented fish sauce, wine, and a scattering of rare, prized peppercorns, as suggested by the Roman cookery writer Apicius.

But in either the rustic farmhouse or the palatial mansion in town, the sound of pestle upon mortar signaled the creation of something good to eat. Etruscan cooks knew that, for all such recipes, the secret of success lay in the rhythm with which the ingredients were pounded. In the painting of the Leinie family's kitchen, a piper stands behind the boy at the mortar, playing the tune that would set the proper beat.

The head chef himself, probably as temperamental as any of his modern counterparts, is also visible, proudly holding high a casserole—no doubt containing his most famous dish. He keeps a wary eye on the underling beside him, who carefully slides a pan into or out of a gaping oven.

Elsewhere, the pressure is mounting, as dinnertime grows near. A maidservant runs across the kitchen carrying two vessels containing something urgently needed by the cooks, while an elegantly dressed woman busily directs another slave to hustle the little service tables into the dining room. Perhaps she is urging him to take care, for these tables are already stacked with round pancakes, fruit—including a pomegranate and black grapes—hard-boiled eggs, and some sort of sweet or spicy morsels. On a nearby wall, men stock up an ancient version of the bar. One struggles under the weight of an ornate covered decanter; others assemble a variety of cups and goblets holding liquids of red or yellow hue, perhaps different kinds of wine. It looks as if the Leinie household was preparing for a long and strenuously sociable night.

An example of Etruscan bronze-workers' craftsmanship, this fifth-century-BC incense burner is supported by an ecstatic dancer accompanying herself with castanets. Wall paintings depict similar incense burners and candelabra at banquets where loosely clad dancers sometimes performed with the fixtures balanced on their heads.

An Etruscan banquet was not complete without bronze strainers such as this foot-long, fifth-century-BC example, which was used to filter fermentation residues from the wine. The Gorgon design in the center was an ancient but later addition.

For the banquet itself, ample evidence survives. Tombs hold prized collections of bronze kitchen utensils, drinking vessels, and plates, often marked with the names of their owners. Excavations have also yielded thousands of pieces of pottery, ranging from ordinary functional basins and bowls to lavishly decorated specimens of ceramic art, lustrously colored and richly adorned with human and animal figures or fanciful patterns. Wealthy Etruscans were avid collectors of the handsome vases made in Athens and imported them in enormous quantities.

From the food to the utensils to the entertainment provided, Etruscan parties were clearly events of a high aesthetic standard. Scenes depicted on paintings, architectural plaques, and sculpted urns show the elegantly dressed and bejeweled diners reclining on their beautifully draped couches, serving themselves with handfuls of delicacies, summoning servants to pour more wine for yet another toast. The festivities might take place indoors, illuminated by bronze candelabra, or in the open air, surrounded by ribboned and garlanded trees and sheltered by gaily colored awnings. One painting representing such an alfresco occasion even depicted tiny birds hopping on the ground below the diners, seeking out stray, delectable crumbs.

Throughout the evening, men and women danced for the company, moving singly, in pairs, or in lines where each entertainer performed a different set of steps. Some accompanied themselves with castanets, and there were always musicians playing lyres, zithers, straight and curved trumpets, and the Etruscans' most beloved source of sound—the pipe. But neither dance nor music was restricted to such dinner-party entertainments. Dancers also flexed their hands, twirled, kicked, and leapt in ecstatic abandon on ceremonial occasions, such as funerals or religious rites.

Livy, for example, tells the tale of a plague that fell upon Rome during the fourth century BC. Hoping to escape the hardship, the Romans turned to their Etruscan neighbors, who not only provided soothsayers skilled—like the lady Tanaquil of yore—in decoding the hidden messages of the gods, but also sent a corps of performers to soothe the deities who had visited their anger on the city. Probably wearing masks, the artists danced to the sound of the pipe "in the most graceful way imaginable, in the Etruscan fashion, their movements unaccompanied by either singing or dramatic action."

According to the Roman author Aelianus, writing in the third

95

century AD, Etruscans also used music when hunting to lure stags and wild boars from their hiding places. "Nets," he reported, "are stretched out, and all kinds of traps are set in position in a circle. A skilled piper then plays the sweetest tunes the double pipe can produce, avoiding the shriller notes. The quiet and the stillness carry the sounds, and the music floats up into all the lairs and resting places of the animals. At first the animals are terrified. But later they are irresistibly overcome by the enjoyment of the music. Spellbound, they are gradually attracted by the powerful music and, forgetting their young and their homes, they draw near, bewitched by the sounds, until they fall, overpowered by the melody, into the snares."

Hunting, with or without music, was as much a pleasant pastime for the Etruscan rich as it was a vital source of protein for the rural peasantry. In Tarquinia, a clan of outdoorsmen commemorated their sporting enthusiasms on the painted walls of a burial chamber known as the Tomb of Hunting and Fishing. They are shown on horseback enjoying the company of their gamboling dogs after a good day's hunt, while their servants, on foot, shoulder the weight of the kill. Elsewhere, in an idyllic landscape near an azure sea, boys dive into the water or climb a grassy cliff *(page 38)*, while their companions, in boats, spear fish or catch them with nets, hook, and line *(pages 100-101)*.

In the towns, public spectacles such as competitive games and chariot races marked religious festivals and provided holiday entertainment for the crowds. In Etruria, as in Greece and later in Rome, games were also performed as part of the funeral rites for important personages. On plaques and bowls for religious offerings, as well as on the painted walls of tombs, thrilling episodes from these events are frozen and replayed for all eternity.

Onlookers cram onto wooden reviewing stands and, shielded by awnings from the fierce Italian sun, watch jugglers, dancers, and acrobats or cheer on their favorite teams of horses and riders. Drivers flash whips over the backs of straining horses almost flying over the ground, and on a tomb painting at Tarquinia, a fallen horse whinnies in panic as it struggles to free its legs from a tangle of reins.

At Tarquinia also, a burial chamber known as the Tomb of the Two-Horse Chariots records the tense moments before the start of a race—the excited, chattering crowd, horses being yoked, a procession of chariots making its way toward the starting line. Yet the chariot contest is only one of several simultaneous events under way at

this painted arena. Nearby, umpires scrutinize wrestlers and boxers with an expert and critical eye, while other athletes warm up in readiness for vaulting, foot races, or the discus throw.

Because of the Etruscans' enthusiasm for portraying themselves in these and other moments of their lives, scholars have a record of the clothes they wore and of the ways these fashions changed during the centuries when their civilization was at its height. Style, then as now, was never static. Only gods and goddesses, perhaps to express their timeless, unchanging nature, were represented in garments of archaic cut; apart from the priests and priestesses who served the cults, most mortals were enthusiastic followers of fashion.

It would have been impossible for Etruscans to remain impervious to the stylistic influences from the eastern side of the Adriatic Sea, and Etruscan art and design, especially after the middle of the sixth century BC, reflects all manner of Greek and Oriental touches. Yet the clothing worn by real people, as distinct from many of the figures revealed only in works of art, displayed features that marked their owners as Etruscans rather than Greeks. In the seventh century BC, for example, a popular sandal with hinged wooden soles inches thick was often put in the grave. Sandals with thin gold laces were called "Etruscan sandals" in Athens and either imported as a luxury item from Etruria or copied. Even more distinctively Etruscan was a laced leather shoe with an upturned, pointed toe. Long after mortal men and women had abandoned it, it remained the standard footwear for goddesses in art.

Etruscans, perhaps because of Italy's cooler climates, dressed in heavier

These sixth-century-BC, 10-inch-long wooden-soled sandals from Bisenzio had bronze hinges to make them flexible. Etruscan footwear was famed throughout the ancient world. Gold-laced shoes, for example, were popular among fashionable Athenian women.

97

fabrics than their Greek contemporaries and instead of loose draperies, sometimes constructed their garments from pieces of fabric sewed together and tailored to fit. Greeks opted for elegant simplicity; Etruscans preferred their costumes more elaborately decorated, with ornate accessories such as belts, jewelry, and hats in a variety of shapes—petaled, melon-shaped, twisted, or rising to a point.

For the Greek philosopher Posidonius, the Etruscan appetite for luxurious clothes and dazzling jewelry was yet another proof of moral decadence. He noted with particular disapproval that Etruscans allowed even their slaves to dress flamboyantly. Other commentators reported that some fashions were, at times, adopted enthusiastically by both sexes: Draped mantles that were the precursors to the Roman toga, certain types of footwear, and short hair styles were cases in point.

Such permissiveness would have seemed even more appalling to the Romans, with their rigid dress codes. Unlike the Etruscans, who apparently wore whatever suited them, Rome assigned garments or modes of decoration to specific social classes, genders, and age groups as marks of identification and badges of status. The toga, for example, denoted Roman citizenship and was therefore worn only by men. So when Roman historians viewed surviving representations of Etruscans in their togalike robes, they concluded—wrongly—that the women of Etruria dressed in men's clothing.

Despite such misconceptions, many details of Etruscan dress from the sixth and fifth century BC would survive throughout the Roman republic and even into the imperial age. The styles were preserved in the official garments worn by magistrates and priests and were proudly legitimized by Roman antiquarians as harking back to the ancient days of the "Etruscan kings."

The lavish costumes and intricate jewelry so beloved by aristocratic Etruscans did not come cheaply. Etruria must have been a rich land indeed to afford the treasures and pleasures displayed in the tombs of the elite. Even after the Etruscan cities had lost their independence and come under the sway of Rome, they still had wealth to spare.

When the Roman general Scipio Africanus embarked on his campaign against Carthage in 205 BC, for instance, Etruscan towns contributed materials for the war effort. According to a list compiled by Livy, Arezzo offered helmets, shields, and spears in the thousands,

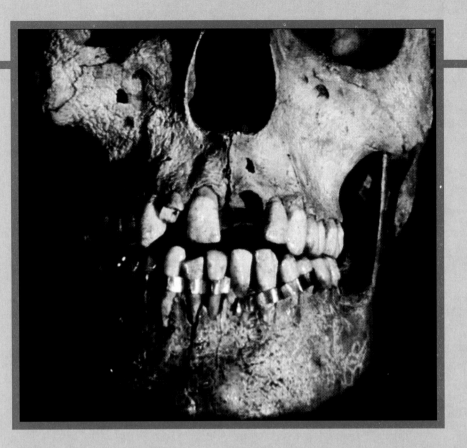

ETRUSCAN DENTISTRY: THE ALLURE OF A GLITTERING SMILE

The Etruscans are famous for their impressive tombs, bridges, roads, and irrigation systems. But the area in which they were probably the furthest ahead of their time is dentistry.

Archaeological excavations of tombs have revealed just how ingenious and advanced these ancient dentists were. They used modified calf and oxen teeth, bone, and ivory, often fastened with tiny pegs, to make dentures and crowns. Bridges, an Etruscan invention, were made from extremely soft gold by skilled goldsmiths. These malleable appliances were then fixed above the gumline, supported by oth-

er teeth, to avoid undue discomfort for their wearers.

Curiously, all Etruscan skulls discovered so far containing bridgework have belonged to females, such as that above with its two finely wrought examples (the longer bridge has slipped down from its original position). Experts think gold dental appliances were something of a status symbol. The size and prominence of the goldwork found suggests that some bridges were

worn for cosmetic purposes, although these would also have held loose teeth in place.

The technological advances made by the dentists were to be lost once the Etruscans were assimilated into the early Roman Republic and their dental knowledge faded into the same oblivion as their culture.

Indeed, no gold bridgework has been found from the periods of the republic and empire. Yet so high was the quality of Etruscan work of almost 3,000 years ago that it would not be surpassed until the 1870s, when dentistry can be said to have entered the modern age.

as well as enough axes, sickles, spades, baskets, and handmills to furnish 40 ships of the fleet. The sails for these vessels came from cloth provided by the linen weavers of Tarquinia, and iron was sent from the mines at Populonia. The towns known today as Perugia, Volterra, Roselle, and Chiusi sent pitch, pine, and hardwoods to build ships for the invasion force and grain to feed the troops. More foodstuffs came from Cerveteri.

Field surveys conducted near the small town of Tuscania, about 50 miles northwest of Rome, between 1986 and 1990 have suggested that such large cities were fed by a complex assortment of rural hamlets and major and minor farms. From early times these homesteads had grown wheat, barley, and millet in rotation with such legumes as peas and lentils. In the middle of the first millennium BC, the cultivation of olives and grapes also became profitable. Although imperial Romans would not rate Etruscan wine very high—the poet Martial complained that it was too light for his liking—the locals seem to have taken to it with enthusiasm, since Greek writers as early as the fourth century BC felt impelled to note that heavy drinking was an Etruscan habit common to both sexes.

The tomb paintings rarely show scenes of farming life, but documentary sources give some flavor of Etruscan life on the land. According to Columella, a first-century-AD Roman writer on agrarian matters, farmers worked the fields behind plows pulled by oxen that were lean but had considerable stamina for hard work. Along with cattle, pigs were reared as a prime source of meat, and their slaughter seemed to have been an essential precursor to ancient rites, such as the celebration of a princely marriage. The second-century-BC Greek historian Polybius described the unique methods of Etruscan swineherds: Instead of walking behind their pigs to keep them moving, they led their charge from the front, blowing a trumpet to produce a note or tune that the pigs would recognize and follow.

Even in Roman times, Etruscans were respected for their agricultural expertise. Two important writers on farming matters in the second century BC were Saserna the Elder and Saserna the Younger, a father and son of Etruscan origins with strong views about the ideal farm based on their own experience. They extolled the notion of a small, self-sufficient agricultural unit with a highly organized work force. Little or nothing would be brought in from outside—even the tools for working the land and the containers for storing the food it produced should be made on the premises. The excavation of a farm

Perhaps reflecting the sporting interest of its occupant, this detail from a sixth-century-BC fresco in the Tomb of Hunting and Fishing at Tarquinia shows fishermen in a boat and a hunter on a cliff using a slingshot to bring down birds in flight. One of the few Etruscan depictions of fishing, the painting underscores the importance of seafood in the diet, as revealed by the number of fish bones found at excavation sites.

in the Viterbo region, more or less contemporary with the Sasernas, could almost be seen as a model of their principles put into practice, equipped even with a kiln for making terra-cotta plaques and tiles to adorn its buildings.

Etruscans were also expert engineers, building canals, tapping subterranean water sources, and draining swamps and lakes. In this, they were spurred on by the will to make the best use of their land, and by a desire to include water in the rituals they conducted at their rural sanctuaries. The most dramatic archaeological evidence of their skills comes from southern Etruria. Here they cut deep into the soft volcanic rock to create underground passages—cuniculi—that would convey water from one valley to another, draining off the excess from one area and redirecting it elsewhere. In order to gain access to these channels, they dug vertical shafts with ladderlike steps carved into their walls.

Etruscans also built a network of roads and bridges. Archaeological evidence suggests that these developments coincided with the influx of imported goods in the seventh and sixth centuries BC and the appearance of wheeled vehicles to transport them. Testaments to the determination of Etruscan engineers to create the easiest possible route for cart and wagon traffic, the roads wind their way down the steep sides of valleys and, in places, pass through enormous trenches hewn from rocky hillsides. Bridges ranged from simple wooden planks across a ford to spans supported by massive stone abutments. The planners of these public works seemed sensitive to the needs of town and countryside dwellers alike: Soon after the network linked the major urban centers, branch roads were extended to minor settlements as well.

It is a tantalizing irony that while some of these roadways sur-

A SWEDISH KING'S HOBBY AND PASSION—DIGGING IN THE DIRT

With the gusto that his forebears might have mustered for a battle or a stag hunt, King Gustav VI Adolf of Sweden, in 1957, plunged into a scheme for the excavation of three Etruscan villages at San Giovenale, Luni sul Mignone, and Acquarossa, a trio of sites about 50 miles north of Rome. Under the king's patronage and with his hands-on help, these sites yielded the first substantial evidence of early houses, not of aristocrats, but of Etruria's humbler folk.

The king's infatuation with archaeology had begun at the age of 15, in 1898, when he applied a pickax and spade to a spot near his summer palace where it was said that there were ancient burials. He did indeed find an Iron Age tomb and a few objects. From then on his delight in digging never waned, and in 1926 he founded the Swedish Archaeological Institute in Rome. Over his lifetime he participated in more than 30 different excavations.

After he was told of the Etruscan sites by an official of his court, topographer Eric Wetter, the king raised funds for the project. Every October, for 15 seasons until his death at 92 in 1973, he moved into on-site quarters, often with his wife, Queen Louise, and his grandchildren, including Margrethe, the future queen of Denmark. During his stay he used the alias "the count of Gripsholm." Subordinating himself to the excavation leaders, he brought his experience and technical skills to bear on the painstaking daily operations.

In a valley thick with ancient tombs, the bespectacled King Gustav VI Adolf, seated at the head of the table, hosts an open-air luncheon (left) near San Giovenale. Among his guests are luminaries of Etruscan studies, invited to exchange views with the Swedish and Italian experts on the team. In the background, the entrance to a tomb is visible.

Shirt sleeves rolled up, the king probes occupation levels of a seventh- to sixth-century village at San Giovenale (above). His granddaughter, Princess Margrethe of Denmark (above, right), stands in a chamber tomb holding artifacts found there. At lower right, the king sketches a floor plan of an Etruscan house uncovered in San Giovenale. His 1963 drawing, shown below, is annotated in Swedish.

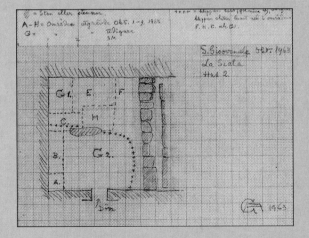

vive, many of the great towns they connected are today virtually impossible to excavate. These settlements lie sealed below layer upon layer of some 2,000 years of active urban life, with its endless progression of demolition and rebuilding; the areas are often still inhabited. But in the 1950s, Italian archaeologists, through an extraordinary conjunction of luck, dedication, and a bit of double-dealing, learned the whereabouts of a vanished but still eminently accessible Etruscan city, ripe for rediscovery and excavation.

To some cynics within the world of classical archaeology, the lost Etruscan city of Spina, a great trading port on the Adriatic Sea, was nothing but a myth, a northern Italian version of fabled Atlantis. But the Italian archaeologist Nereo Alfieri suspected that the lagoons at the silted-up mouth of the river Po hid much more—traces of a metropolis that from the sixth to the third century BC served as a cosmopolitan meeting place for Etruscans, Greeks, and traders from northern Italy, the East, and other locations.

In Roman times, silt cut Spina off from the sea. The bustling port, with its canals, quays, warehouses, markets, and great public spaces, declined into a sleepy village of the Po Delta and then apparently disappeared altogether. In the 1920s, an eel fisherman from nearby Comacchio—itself a once-thriving maritime city strangled by the silt—pulled from the muddy

A man and his oxen are depicted plowing in this fourth-century-BC bronze votive offering from Arezzo. Archaeologists once thought the work showed a simple farmer tending his fields, but they now believe it illustrates a priest digging a sacred furrow to mark off the boundaries for a new city, as legend says Romulus did when founding Rome.

Some 24 feet high, a fourth-century-BC Etruscan gate survives embedded in Roman masonry at Volterra. Gates like this, with its three distinctive but badly eroded protruding heads, probably representing gods, are often seen in the reliefs on Etruscan cremation urns from the area.

bottom an old bucchero pot that antiquities dealers recognized as Etruscan. In no time, more fragments, including many beautiful red-figured Greek pieces, began to turn up on the black market.

Archaeologists soon found the reason for their sudden appearance. A government drainage project had lowered the water level of the surrounding marshes, revealing the remains of a huge Etruscan cemetery. Excavators found 1,250 tombs and a rich store of grave goods, ranging from golden earrings and Egyptian perfume bottles to Athenian vases.

Such a vast, well-furnished necropolis could only have existed to serve a large and prosperous population. But to the frustration of Alfieri, decades of excavation had failed to uncover any signs of a city. Year after year, he fruitlessly combed ancient manuscripts for clues to Spina's location, dug test holes in the marsh that turned up nothing, and eagerly watched as more lagoons were drained. But when the waters disappeared, they left behind only a blank expanse of mud flat.

Then, in 1953, Etruscan artifacts reappeared on the black market. A lagoon lying a few miles to the south, the Valle Pega, had been drained enough for treasure hunters to find their quarry. Working in eel boats at night, they probed the muck with steel-tipped poles and dug wherever they struck something hard. Archaeologists later found tombs the looters missed, including one containing the skeleton of a woman buried with a gold brooch and a necklace of Baltic amber. But Spina itself remained elusive until the spring of 1956, when the Valle Pega, finally drained completely, sprouted a cover of new plant life.

Aerial photographs revealed the pattern of something lying

beneath it: a grid of canals, including one central waterway some 60 feet wide, and rectangular blocks that seemed to mark the sites of scores of vanished buildings. To Alfieri, the colored shapes could be nothing other than the remains of the metropolis of Spina.

Exploring the sandy soil between the canals, the archaeologist found wooden piles resembling those that support the floating city of Venice and, among the props, fragments of pottery that proved the antiquity of the site: Experts concurred that they dated no later than the fifth century BC. "All my doubts dissolved," declared Alfieri. Spina had risen from its watery grave.

Archaeologists later found enormous amounts of Greek pottery, including many pieces from Athens and the colonies in southern Italy, along with jewelry and bronzes crafted in Etruria, faience from the East, and more amber. The artifacts attest to the considerable volume of commerce from which Spina once drew its vigor. In fact, so much Athenian pottery has been recovered that scholars have been able to use it to track the output and creative progress of specific artists—masters and pupils alike—in fifth-century-BC Greece.

Excavations conducted at nearby Marzabotto, a city on the Reno River about 12 miles southwest of Bologna, have yielded similar insights into the influence of the Greek grid layout on Etruscan town planning. A main thoroughfare almost 50 feet wide ran from north to south and was intersected by three avenues that were aligned east and west. Narrower streets were laid parallel to the

Eel fishermen such as the ones in this 1930 photograph discovered the burial grounds of the lost Etruscan city of Spina in 1922, when the water level of marshes of the Po Delta dropped and they hauled up hoards of bucchero pots. More than 1,000 tombs and hundreds of sarcophagi, including the one at right, were to emerge from the mud during the 1930s excavations.

north-south axis, forming a grid of rectangular city blocks reminiscent of the ones found in the Greek cities of the Aegean and their colonies in southern Italy.

Archaeologists excavating within the blocks at Marzabotto were able to discover the foundations of buildings. Though plans varied, many featured a broad passageway that led from the street to a central courtyard, around which were arranged a series of rooms. Water was either fetched from a well sunk in the courtyard or transported from a cistern located on a nearby hillside via round terra-cotta pipes, some of which were recovered among the foundations. Drainage ditches along the streets carried off waste.

Commercial buildings apparently were not segregated from residences. In fact, some structures seemed to have been designed so that their owners could work and sleep under the same roof. Identified as metal workshops because of the stone weights, tools, and slag they contained, several structures along the north-south axis had what appeared to be business rooms on the street side and private quarters around the courtyard.

Judging from such remains, scholars have concluded that the people of Marzabotto, like those of Spina, were merchants rather than warriors. Indeed, a low acropolis that overlooks Marzabotto to the northwest had only a handful of religious structures on its top, and no ramparts or battlements, and scholars have commented on the scarcity of weaponry among the finds excavated from Spina. Its residents may have considered their canals, thick with ships, as sufficient defense against invasion from the sea. But when danger did arrive, probably in the form of an invading army of Gauls, sweeping westward over northern Italy, it came by land, and the peaceable traders were taken by surprise.

The military subjects illustrated in the tombs suggest that Etruscans did have some kind of warrior caste or soldierly tradition. Roman tradition even holds that they were the first Italians to fight in the tight-knit battle formation known as the phalanx. But little is known for sure of the wars they waged, and there is no convincing archaeological evidence of the way they organized their fighting forces. Rather, scholars can only base assumptions on scattered artifacts discovered in tombs, including one that came to light by accident in 1823, when Carlo Avvolta, the chief magistrate of Tarquinia and a longtime amateur Etruscologist, was supervising a road-repair project within his territory.

Needing some stones for the enterprise, Avvolta had his workers dig into a rocky mound at the roadside. In no time, they came upon masonry, which Avvolta followed until he recognized the center of the ceiling of an Etruscan burial chamber. After a hole was made, he peered in and saw what for him was the find of a lifetime: a golden crown shining out of the darkness. A closer look revealed that the diadem rested upon a stone table opposite a man clad in full armor, stretched out upon a bed also hewn from rock. Nearby lay traces of charred bones, the remnants of some sacrificial offering, and a set of weapons—a lance, eight javelins, round shields of bronze, a double-edge sword with a cross-shaped hilt.

But as Avvolta contemplated this extraordinary discovery, something strange and terrible took place. "The body," he reported, "became agitated with a sort of trembling, heaving motion (which lasted a few minutes) and then quickly disappeared, dissolved by contact with the air."

Unfortunately for future scholars, the warrior's surviving grave goods soon vanished as well. Some Avvolta himself gave away, others were sold to collectors who mixed them with items from other tombs, thereby masking their provenance, and an unknown quantity were stolen when a passing thunderstorm forced Avvolta and his colleagues to stop excavating. When they returned to work, the artifacts were gone. The crown that had initially caught Avvolta's eye was luckily spared. But made of heavily corroded bronze covered with thin gold plate, it crumbled away while being transported to Rome.

As a result, Avvolta's vision of military pomp and grandeur remains one piece of a large puzzle: No literature survives to record Etruria's way of waging war. Foreign commentators on the Etruscan character make no mention of soldierly virtues or the lust for battle. Yet the greatest threat to the Etruscan civilization, the likely cause of its disappearance, was the inexorable rise and forceful expansion of neighboring Rome.

HOUSES OF THE OTHER WORLD

The Etruscans not only enjoyed life to its fullest, but for most of their history, they envisioned a rich afterlife for themselves as well. Accordingly, they created lavish tombs modeled on their homes, often complete with household effects—including beds, chairs, footstools, and of course, food and drink.

Their concern for creating living space for the spirit appeared first in Villanovan-period cinerary urns. As containers for the ashes of the deceased, they were lovingly produced in the form of everyday shelters. The ninth-century-BC ceramic urn shown above, although less than 14 inches tall, is embellished with a wealth of architectural details: Interlocking wooden beams hold down the thatched roof, a small hole beneath the eaves lets out smoke, the door opens and closes, and lively geometrical patterns decorate the circular walls. Such urns were buried in well-like graves, along with household goods or prized possessions the dead might need.

The modest hut urns foreshadowed the develop-

ment of the great chamber tombs that dominated Etruscan cemeteries after the Villanovan period. For people who could afford them, these tombs increasingly came to resemble the dwellings of the aristocracy. Their bodies were now interred, rather than cremated, and this freed architects from the constraints of miniaturization, enabling them to create elaborate interiors. Life-size ceramic or stone sarcophagi, lovingly shaped in the likenesses of the occupants, were laid in the tombs, with items the dead would need for housekeeping displayed nearby.

In areas where cremation continued as a custom, to become popular once again toward the end of the Etruscan era, cinerary urns—often complete with portraits of those whose ashes they held—were placed in the chamber tombs. Fittingly, the Etruscans' homes for the dead have outlasted their more ephemeral shelters for the living by millennia and may remain for thousands of years to come.

Although the Etruscans left almost no written records of their beliefs concerning death, the care with which they constructed their tombs lets visitors see how they lived—and how much they expected to enjoy the next life. In addition to the paintings on the walls of many of the tombs, the furnishings reveal some of the comforts to which well-to-do Etruscans had become accustomed.

The structure of the chamber tombs probably is a reproduction of the floor plans of the aristocratic houses of the day. In one popular arrangement, a long, sloping passage called a *dromos* leads down into the tomb and is flanked by two small rooms. Just beyond these lies a wide main chamber, frequently containing several funerary beds positioned against the walls. At the rear, doors, and sometimes windows,

open onto three small, parallel rooms that hold additional beds. An entire family would typically share these accommodations, resting peacefully together, as they did in life.

In Cerveteri's Tomb of the Shields and Chairs (below), carved from tufa, a soft volcanic rock, jambs and lintels frame the doorways, shields hang from the walls, and curved armchairs come complete with footstools.

In the Tomb of the Alcove at Cerveteri (above), a married couple's burial couch is sheltered in a raised niche flanked by twin fluted columns, just as their bed may have been in life. The square, massive pillars appear separate from the ceiling but are in fact joined to it, having been cut from the surrounding tufa.

Delicately carved capitals like this one atop a faceted column lend their name to Cerveteri's Tomb of the Capitals. The funeral couches hug the walls under a ceiling cut to imitate beams and planking. Here, too, the entire space has been hollowed out of the tufa.

Creature comforts—ranging from pillows to the slippers sitting on the rail of the right-hand bed—are preserved in affectionate detail in the painted stucco reliefs of the Matunas family tomb, or the Tomb of the Reliefs, at Cerveteri. Nothing has been overlooked by way of homey detail, including two household animals, the marten and goose, which are visible at lower left.

IN DEATH NOT DIVIDED

Intimacy and equality between husband and wife constitute one of the most extraordinary facets of Etruscan society. The open display of emotion between partners, which shocked Greek and Roman writers enough for them to have written about it at some length, is celebrated and commemorated in the artful images of loving couples that decorate numerous sarcophagi and cinerary urns.

Etruscan artists often embraced stylistic influences from over the sea. For example, the two life-size sarcophagi shown here both display strong Greek elements in the treatment of bodies and faces but are of different periods, one early, one late. However, each artist has molded the foreign style to suit the Etruscan taste, reveling in moments of marital affection and intimacy that are rarely depicted in Greek art.

As though conversing with guests, a sixth-century-BC husband and wife (below) *are shown reclining on a banquet couch. Even their feet convey their relaxed mood, his shoeless, hers clad in fashionable slippers* (inset). *The couple's upturned palms may once have held food or, in the man's case, a* patera, *or saucer into which priests or visitors might have poured libations of wine.*

The fourth-century-BC sarcophagus at right depicts husband Larth Tetnies and wife Thanchvil Tarnai embracing in bed, their bodies draped lightly by a sheet, their gazes locked for all eternity.

The somber atmosphere of the later tombs seems not just to reflect the sorrowful passing of individual lives but to anticipate the decline of Etruscan life itself as Rome gained ascendancy over Etruria. The Romans saw death not as a continuation of a light-hearted existence, filled with banquets and other pleasures, but as a terrifying journey by boat to the underworld, guided by the grim ferryman Charon.

The Etruscans called him Charun and gave him a mighty hammer, then added their own demon, Tuchulcha, equipped with a vulture's beak and serpents, as his fearsome assistant.

Especially in northern Etruria, where cremation persisted, many tombs became repositories for urns containing the ashes of entire generations of families. Though some tombs continued to be constructed in the form of houses, others were void of architectural embellishment and homey details. No longer friendly abodes of joy and celebration they had become frightening places inhabited by demons as well as the dead.

Rows of cinerary urns, originally 53 in all, line the walls of the Inghirami tomb (below), unearthed near Volterra in 1861. Since then, the Florence Archeological Museum moved the tomb and rebuilt it in the museum gardens.

Members of the Volumnii family lie in this magnificent tomb near Perugia that re-creates the grandeur of their aristocratic homes. The atrium, with its ridged roof and decorative reliefs including a shield and swords, leads to other chambers where generations of the family, dating from the second and first centuries BC, were laid to rest in urns that often bore portraits of the dead.

Known as I Vecchi, or The Old Folks, the first-century-BC urn below realistically portrays an older couple. Their expressions are sad, seemingly in recognition of life's passage. Some scholars have another interpretation of the piece, however: They suggest that the woman is a female demon, come to lead the man to the other world.

THE DARKER SIDE OF A PROUD PEOPLE

Produced in the sixth century BC and heavily influenced by Ionian models, this life-size terra-cotta figure of Apollo, or Aplu to the Etruscans, once adorned the rooftop of a temple at Veii. It is thought to be the work of Vulca, the only Etruscan artist whose name has come down to modern times.

The stairway, seven broad steps attached to a huge burial mound at the foot of the hilltop city of Cortona, would have sent a shiver up any worshiper's spine. On either side of the stairway are two sculpted stone blocks, each depicting a sphinx clasping a kneeling warrior in its claws. Each man is burying a knife in his attacker's side, and each warrior's head is all but engulfed in a monster's mouth. Locked, literally and symbolically, in a struggle between life and death, the figures are a reminder, if any mortal ever needs reminding, that there is no escaping fate, that every human effort to elude the grasp of death is doomed.

For Paola Zamarchi Grassi and her fellow archaeologists, who began work at the site in the late 1980s, these macabre sculptures, intriguing echoes of a motif often encountered in the distant lands of the Middle East, were less interesting overall than the steps they framed and the platform the steps led up to. Earlier explorers had already established that a funerary complex comprising the adjacent tumulus and two others stood west of the city. The discoverer of the famed François Vase *(pages 56-57)*, the Italian Etruscologist Alessandro François, had excavated one of these in 1842 and been rewarded for his efforts with the discovery of an Etruscan burial chamber. Inside lay a funeral bed, hewn from volcanic rock, adorned with a relief of eight grief-stricken women. Nearly a century later, in 1928, the

Italian archaeologist Antonio Minto opened part of a second tumulus across a stream and about 300 yards from the one excavated by Grassi and found the final resting places of Etruscan aristocrats.

Only Grassi's, however, included a platform and steps. Because they did not reach the top of the mound, and because they showed little signs of wear, she and her colleagues surmised that they must have played a ritual role, not a practical one. Indeed, a similar raised platform with stairs discovered at the Greek city of Miletus, on the coast of present-day Turkey, was dedicated to the god Poseidon and is known to have served as a gathering place and an altar. Considering the extensive contacts the Etruscans had with Greeks from Asia Minor at the time, in the sixth century BC, Grassi figured that the stairs she had unearthed probably had a comparable function: They led up to an open-air altar at which Cortona's residents paid homage to their exalted dead and perhaps performed some rite meant to assist the passing of the eternal soul from the corruptible body.

Grassi's discovery is valuable because the Etruscans were known in ancient times to be an especially devout people. Like the Greeks and Romans, they regarded the sacred and the secular as one and the will of the gods as paramount. But whereas the Greeks used logic as a stepstool to set themselves on a more equal footing with their gods,

After using pumps to drain water from the sodden site, archaeologists were rewarded when they found these remarkably well preserved steps leading up to an open-air altar. Constructed during the sixth century BC at Cortona, the altar, some 16 feet wide, was most likely used during cult ceremonies and funeral processions.

and the Romans devised a body of laws to help them master the unknown forces around them, the Etruscans reserved center stage exclusively for the gods and took their places humbly in the wings. There they listened to, but never played an active role in, their capricious deities' performances, which they understood to be monologues, not dialogues.

"There is this difference between us Romans and Etruscans," observed Nero's tutor, the philosopher Seneca, in the first century AD. "We believe that lightning is caused by clouds colliding, whereas they believe that clouds collide in order to create lightning. Since they attribute everything to the gods, they are led to believe, not that events have a meaning because they have happened, but that they happen in order to express a meaning."

If to the rational Seneca such phenomena were nothing more than natural, to the Etruscans they were nothing less than signs from the gods. Deciphering those signs was the key to understanding the will of the gods, and thus divination—that is, the interpretation of lightning bolts, the passing by of flocks of birds, and other events, as well as the reading of livers and other internal organs—lay at the heart of the Etruscan religion. Out of their observation of the world around them, the Etruscans created a quasi-science whose tenets, they believed, could be used to predict the future.

According to the first-century-BC Roman statesman and author Cicero, one of several writers to tell the tale, the science was inspired by Tages, a mysterious child who looked like an old man. Said to be the grandson of the god Jupiter, he sprang from a freshly plowed furrow in Tarquinia. Amazed, the plowman gave a great cry, and soon "the whole of Etruria assembled at the spot," including a man named Tarchon, the city-state's legendary founder. He asked Tages a series of questions. Answering with wisdom that belied his youth, the boy expounded on the mysteries of life and divulged the secrets of divination while the Etruscans listened eagerly and wrote down all that was said. Then, as suddenly as he appeared, the boy-seer vanished.

Along with the truths revealed by other

Unique in Etruscan funerary art, this much-eroded stone sculpture of a warrior battling a sphinx is one of two such carvings that decorate the altar at Cortona. The sphinx—perhaps representing a demon of death—grasps the kneeling warrior in her huge paws, while the warrior, wearing a pleated tunic, buries his dagger in her flank.

prophets, including a nymph named Vegoia who is said to have shared "the decisions of Jupiter and of Justice" with the lucumo of Clusium, Tages's message became the foundation for a tradition that lasted for centuries. No one can say for sure what the Etruscans called their doctrine, which was recorded in a number of sacred books long since disappeared. But the Romans' Latin label for it was the *disciplina etrusca*, or the Etruscan science. It consisted of three broad categories of texts: the *Libri haruspicini*, a guide to divination using animal entrails; the *Libri fulgurales*, containing the rubrics for interpreting lightning; and the *Libri rituales*, which dealt with the formalities of rituals by which cities were founded, temples and altars consecrated, and armies organized. To these were often added the *Libri acherontici*, which described the pathways the dead followed in the afterlife, and the *Libri fatales*, which explained destiny as the Etruscans understood it.

Some scholars think the Etruscans may have originally conceived of a single, supreme deity that revealed itself through several manifestations. Later, under the influence of Greek literature and art, these aspects were given their own identities and human forms, while a number of Greek gods were also introduced. As a result, the Etruscan pantheon was soon crowded with a collection of Greek divinities, Etruscan deities identified with Greek gods, and a panoply of obscure, indigenous supernatural beings.

Etruscologists know the names of many of these deities. The names appear in inscriptions on surviving Etruscan monuments and on the backs of engraved mirrors bearing mythological scenes, as well as in such fragmentary texts as the so-called Capua tile, an inscribed terra-cotta roofing piece dating to the fifth century BC, and the Zagreb mummy book *(page 25)*. But they are best presented on the so-called Liver of Piacenza *(page 127)*, an inscribed, life-size model of a

Clutching a thunderbolt, the stylized, fifth-century-BC bronze figure at left represents the Etruscan sky god Tinia. Like the Greek Zeus, Tinia was a powerful deity, with lightning interpreted as a celestial warning from him. The goddess Menerva—similarly rendered in exaggerated fashion in the bronze at right—was worshiped in sanctuaries throughout Etruria. Though usually dressed in warrior garb, as here, she was a fertility deity associated with procreation and childbirth.

sheep's liver that around 100 BC or earlier may have been used to train the chosen few who read the entrails of sacrificed animals to discern the will of the gods.

A farmer unearthed the bronze object near the northern city of Piacenza, south of Milan, in 1877. Unaware of the object's great value to Etruscologists, he at first tossed it under a tree but later retrieved it and sold it for a pittance to his parish priest, thus starting a long odyssey from conversation piece to museum piece: The priest, who planned to keep the artifact only as a curiosity, changed his mind and sold it at a sizable profit after the liver had the unintended effect of rousing the interest of a landowner with a fondness for antiquities.

Neither the new owner nor any of the collectors and antiquarians to whom he showed it recognized the bronze liver for what it was. Indeed, by the time the object finally found its way into the local museum in Piacenza in 1894, only one expert, allegedly an authority on things Etruscan, had come close to identifying it as a liver. Not until 1905, some 28 years after it had been harvested from a furrow, did a German scholar make the connection between it and a real sheep's liver.

The outer ring of the model was divided by engraved lines into 16 rectangular compartments inscribed with the names of various gods. The names of additional deities were etched into 24 inner compartments. Although some of these gods are unique to Etruria, others have their parallels in the Greek and Roman pantheons. Tin, or Tinia, for example, the most important Etruscan god, has his counterpart in the Greek Zeus and the Roman Jupiter; similarly, Uni can be compared to Hera and Juno, Turan to Aphrodite and Venus, and Menerva to Athena and Minerva.

That the deities' names appear on a liver, and not some other part of the body, is of dramatic importance. To the Etruscans, the liver was not just a vital organ, but the seat of life and the regulator of emotions. It was, moreover, a microcosm that mirrored the macrocosm of the heavens. Indeed, most of the deities inscribed on the liver correspond to gods that—according to Martianus Capella, a writer and lawyer born in Carthage in the fifth century AD, and other Latin scholars—governed sectors of the Etruscan heavens.

Capella wrote that the Etruscans envisioned the dome of the sky as a sacred space, what the Romans would later call a templum. They partitioned the heavens according to the precise rules of their science: First the sky was quartered by two straight lines that touched the cardinal points of the compass and crossed overhead at right angles. Then it was subdivided into a total of 16 celestial regions, each the domain of a particular god, that bade well or ill depending upon their location. The east, for instance, the direction of the morning sun, was considered favorable, whereas the west was unfavorable.

Space and time were similarly organized in the Etruscan sphere of things, and the life expectancies of people, nations, and even the universe were considered preordained and immutable. The universe, for example, was allotted a life span of 12 *chiliads*, or roughly 12,000 years, while Etruria merited 10 *saecula*, or ages—periods of unequal length that archaeologists reckon began in the 11th or 10th century BC and were measured in the lifetimes of those persons who survived the longest from one saeculum to the next. According to the *Libri rituales*, the useful period of any man's life was limited to a maximum of 84 years, after which he was no longer capable of receiving messages from the gods and was thus out of sync with the divine order.

Vel Saties, a nobleman from the fourth century BC, looks toward the heavens as his slave, Arnza, prepares to release a small bird in this detail from the François Tomb at Vulci that housed Saties's remains. The Etruscans—and the Romans after them—believed that by studying the flight of birds they could divine the future.

Like many a modern religion, that of the Etruscans was a revealed religion, a faith governed by elaborate rituals and shepherded by a powerful priesthood drawn from the ranks of the aristocracy. The most important members of this royal priesthood were those the Etruscans called *netsvis* and *trutnvt frontac*, but who are known today by their Latin names: *haruspices* and *fulguriatores*. The former divined the will of the gods in the entrails of sacrificed animals, especially the livers of sheep, while the latter observed thunder and lightning and, according to Cicero and Pliny the Elder, could summon lightning with the right combination of prayer and ritual. Other soothsayers, called *avispices*, made predictions based on the flights of birds.

Ostensibly, the jobs of these priests were made easy by the

Found at a sixth-century-BC tomb in Cerveteri, this flat, 14-inch-long bronze is a model of the curved, three-dimensional staff, or lituus, that was carried by members of the powerful Etruscan priesthood as a symbol of their authority. The use of the lituus as a distinctive mark of prestige eventually spread to Rome.

Etruscan propensity for carving *templa* into ritual spaces. Thus, in theory, the fulguriator had only to note from which of the 16 sectors of the sky a bolt of lightning had come, match the sector to its god, and then decide whether the sign augured good or ill. In practice, however, the task was made difficult by the fact that something as simple as the date, the color or shape of a lightning bolt, its trajectory, or its point of impact could alter its meaning. Similar guidelines governed the observation of birds in flight, so the attending avispex carefully noted such variables as the kind of birds, their number, and their position in the sky in relation to the resident gods.

The craft of the haruspex was as demanding and as arcane. He read the livers of only healthy sheep, and then only if they offered no resistance while being led to slaughter. In the early days of the religion, the priest cut out the organ and simply examined its size and color. But later, his craft and that of the fulguriator apparently ran together, as the inscriptions on the Liver of Piacenza indicate, and he read the liver by comparing it with the heavens—that is, the haruspex matched any bump or irregularity in a particular part of the organ with the corresponding sector of the sky and then interpreted it as a sign from the god dwelling there.

If in an age of computer-generated projections the notion of reading a sheep's blood-warm liver for divine messages seems nothing short of bizarre, it was anything but to the fatalistic Etruscans—or, for that matter, to many ancient civilizations. Soothsayers in the Middle East, for instance, and especially in Mesopotamia, read both livers and lightning, as did the Greeks and Romans.

It was in Etruria, however, that these practices assumed what has been called national characteristics. "When the Etruscans had to make a big decision," as Dutch scholar L. Bouke van der Meer put it, "the liver told them go or no go." Indeed, such was the reputation of the liver as an oracle that as early as 304 BC, Roman aristocrats sent their sons to Etruria to study divination, an art considered useful to generals. By the first century BC the Romans had taken to calling the arts of divination, regardless of how the divining was performed or who was doing it, by the single Latin word *haruspicina*.

Like priests of many a time and place, the Etruscan haruspex was outfitted with his own ritual paraphernalia, including a wide knife that was used in the slaughter of sheep and is shown on a bronze statuette slung from the shoulder of a priest. A large sacrificial ax, depicted on the reverse of some Etruscan coins, apparently also numbered among the trappings of the priesthood.

Other artifacts reveal that the haruspex went to work dressed for the occasion or, more accurately, given the nature of his occupation, dressed for the kill. Statuettes and images on coins, gravestones, and the backs of bronze mirrors show him wearing his trademark *pileus*, a tall, conical hat fashioned from the skin of a sacrificed animal. A leather chin strap prevented the hat from toppling off its owner's head in midritual—a bad omen in any haruspex's book. A tunic and a fringed cape, the latter sometimes made from the skin of a sacrificed animal and fastened with a large brooch, usually completed the priest's ritual garb. Some soothsayers are also shown brandishing a *lituus*, the curved stick that was a haruspex's symbol of authority.

Even though the Roman statesman Cato was to remark in the second century BC that it was beyond him how one soothsayer managed to keep a straight face when he met one of his peers, many of his countrymen consulted the Etruscan priests. Even Roman patricians, always of two minds on the value of divination—disdainful of mere superstition, yet fearful of the consequences of ignoring the gods and conscious of the effect on the army—looked to the haruspices for guidance when they found themselves confronted by extraordinary events. The government, too, sought the advice of the priests, as the emperor Claudius I reminded the Roman Senate in AD 47. "It often happened," the Roman historian Tacitus quoted him as saying, "that when the State fell upon evil days, the Etruscan soothsayers were summoned to Rome and ceremonies were revived and thereafter faithfully observed."

Claudius, who was married to an Etruscan woman and wrote a history of Etruria, was hoping to convince the Senate that the study of haruspicina—what he called "the most ancient discipline in Italy"—should be nurtured and that its long-term survival should be ensured by founding a college of 60 officially sanctioned haruspices.

It was owing to such measures that the science outlasted the Etruscan culture and that its practitioners continued to footnote the pages of history for centuries. Earlier, in 44 BC, when an Etruscan haruspex named Spurinna warned a skeptical Julius Caesar to beware the ides of March, the soothsayer also informed him that it would do no good, since his fate had already been irrevocably decreed by the gods. A later emperor, Julian the Apostate, took no chances. When he set out to conquer Asia in the fourth century AD, he brought along a full complement of haruspices. Later still, as Alaric and his fellow Visigoths bore down on Rome in AD 408, Pope Innocent I was said to have enlisted the aid of the haruspices, who offered to pray down a volley of lightning. Whether the soothsayers' prayers fell on deaf ears or whether the pope's faith in such pagan pursuits was something less than wholehearted is impossible to know. What is certain is that Rome was sacked and left for dead by the Visigoths, whose raid did much to hasten the decline of the empire.

In the centuries preceding the birth of the Roman Empire, one of Rome's proudest monuments was the Temple of Jupiter on the city's Capitoline Hill. Although dedicated in 509 BC to the Roman gods

The Etruscan soothsayer's, or haruspex's, ritual garb—seen in the second- or third-century-BC, stylized bronze votive figure at left—included a distinctive conical cap and a fibula to fasten his cloak, since he was not allowed to use knots or strings. One of the haruspex's most important duties was to read entrails to determine the will of the gods. The five-inch-long bronze model of a sheep's liver below, usually dated to about 100 BC and known as the Liver of Piacenza, may once have been used to train novice haruspices in the art of divination.

Jupiter, Juno, and Minerva, the wood and terra-cotta temple was wholly an Etruscan undertaking. Conceived of by the first Etruscan king of Rome, Lucius Tarquinius Priscus, laid out according to the principles of the Etruscan science, constructed by Etruscan laborers and artisans, and built to an Etruscan design—though one adapted from the Greek—it was the largest known Etruscan temple ever erected and perhaps one of the biggest of its time in the classical world. Some of its impressive stone foundation is visible today. According to the Greek historian Dionysius of Halicarnassus, the structure was 168 feet wide and 192 feet deep and once measured 104 feet from the base of its massive podium to the tip of its gabled roof.

The temple represented the culmination of a long evolution in design. The earliest Etruscan places of worship were simple open-air sanctuaries, raised stone platforms where the gods were invoked and their will divined. Ruins of such structures survive at Cortona, on the acropolis overlooking Marzabotto, and at Viterbo, about 40 miles northwest of Rome. A small model, purportedly of an open sanctuary and probably a votive offering, has been found at Chiusi, ancient Clusium.

Sometime in the sixth century BC, however, as the Etruscan gods assumed human forms and as those forms were fashioned into divine images, the roofed temple came into being as a place to shelter them. The remains of a one-room sanctuary unearthed at Veii, the southernmost Etruscan city, 10 miles north of Rome, and numerous terra-cotta models found in tombs indicate that these temples initially consisted of a single chamber, or *cella*. But soon a more elaborate floor plan evolved, and the Etruscan temple assumed the classic form that the Roman architect and engineer Vitruvius was to describe in the first century BC: a box, slightly longer than it was wide, that was divided into halves. A portico, typically consisting of eight columns, stood in front, backed either by three cellae or by a single cella and two open wings.

The Etruscan temple at the height of its development bore more than passing resemblance to its Greek counterpart. The Capitoline temple, for instance, took inspiration for its great size from Greek models in the eastern Mediterranean. And yet there were notable differences: Most important, after the beginning of the sixth century BC, the Greeks started constructing their temples out of stone, while the Etruscans continued to use wood for everything but the foundations.

IS IT REAL? HOW EVEN TWO GREAT MUSEUMS COULDN'T SPOT THE FAKES

To the uninitiated, the sarcophagus below may look Etruscan. In fact, it is a fake produced by two Italian brothers, restorers of Etruscan works. They modeled the piece in the 1860s, then smashed it and buried the fragments in the ground to age them. Dug up, the pieces were sold to an Italian antiques dealer who in turn sold them to the British Museum. One year later a scholar paid the reassembled sarcophagus faint praise, writing: "The style of these figures is archaic, the treatment throughout very naturalistic in which a curious striving after truth in anatomical details gives animation to the group, in spite of extreme ungainliness of form, and ungraceful composition." Could he have been doubting the monument's authenticity? He added, "The inscription is very similar to that of a gold fibula found at Chiusi, but its interpretation is not yet determined."

Though one of the brothers was to admit to having had a hand in the work while the other denied it—and the inscription indeed proved borrowed—the museum remained convinced of its purchase's authenticity and kept the sarcophagus on display for 60 years. Finally, mounting evidence, including the observation that the woman seemed to be dressed in 19th-century underwear, led to its banishment.

The British Museum was not the only institution to be so duped. New York's Metropolitan Museum of Art bought an oversize warrior and placed the figure at the center of its Etruscan collection, where it attracted much attention. The statue turned out to have been made in Italy all right—but in the early 1900s.

A metal frame rises above the ruins of the main temple at Veii to suggest the height and proportions of the original building. Reproduced ornaments line the edge of the roof, and a model of a statue of Apollo sits atop the gable. Rather than re-create the structure, the archaeologists wanted visitors to be able to see the surviving stones unimpeded, hence the architect's use of thin, carefully placed metal rods, airily disposed.

In addition, Greek temples, typically possessing colonnades on all four sides, could be approached from any aspect; Etruscan temples were designed to be entered from one direction only, an architectural convention that dominates many modern classical buildings in cities throughout the world. Laid out according to the dictates of the soothsayers, they frequently faced south and always opened onto an outdoor sanctuary from which priests wanting to get an accurate reading of lightning or birds in flight could take in a wide sweep of open sky. Though Greek temples often had outdoor cult spaces and altars, they had no such adjoining augural area, and their main entrances, like that at the east end of the Parthenon in Athens, usually faced the rising sun.

Etruscan temples were also distinguished by their ornamentation, an architectural flourish they shared with Greek temples, though for different reasons. Greek decorative elements—cornices, friezes, and others—were frequently also crucial parts of the overall structure; the Parthenon's roof, for example, could not be built until the richly carved architrave that ringed the temple had been set in place to support it. On Etruscan temples, the brightly painted terracotta friezes, the fancifully molded antefixes along the eaves, and the revetment plaques on the ends of beams amounted to little more than what one scholar has called "exuberant, wildly colorful afterthoughts." Rather than serving an essential structural function, these elements' purpose was to cover and protect the exposed parts of the wooden superstructure, though they also dressed up the exteriors of the temples.

As a further embellishment, the Etruscans often placed life-size terra-cotta statues, called acroteria, on bases mounted above the slope of a temple's pediments and along the ridge of its roof. These statues were sometimes arranged in settings that depicted religious or symbolic scenes drawn from mythology. Such was the case at one of the most ancient and venerated of all Etruscan temples, the Portonaccio, at Veii.

Here, in 1916, archaeologists combing the temple grounds unearthed a group of statues dating to the sixth century BC that had been carefully buried along the edge of a later Roman road. The statues have as their theme the god Apollo, who was worshiped by both Etruscans and Greeks. Indeed, archaeologists have turned up some 100 votive statuettes of the deity that suggest the main temple may have been dedicated to him and Hercules.

Called by some the most beautiful Etruscan statue ever to have been found, the stunning terra-cotta figure of Apollo emerges from the soil in this photo taken at the moment of its discovery at Veii on May 19, 1916. As archaeologist Giulio Giglioli uncovered the head and shoulders, he was so overcome with emotion that he leaned down and kissed the statue.

One of the terra cottas depicts Apollo as a child: Cradled in the arms of his mother, Latona, he prepares to kill Python, the enormous serpent that, according to myth, hid in the caves of Mount Parnassus and was the terror of the people. Another shows the god *(page 118)* about to grapple with Hercules for control of the deer sacred both to Apollo and to his sister, Diana, the goddess of the moon. Yet another figure, only a fragment of which survives, wears the winged helmet of Mercury. The statues were made at a workshop in Veii by a number of sculptors, perhaps including Vulca, the only Etruscan artist whose name has been recorded.

The ruins of the Portonaccio complex lie just west of Veii, midway between the plateau on which the city sat and the deep valley of the nearby Piordo River, and include the foundations of the temple, an outdoor altar, and a sacred pool, all enclosed by a triangular wall. The temple, possessing a portico in front and three cellae in back, was built around 510 BC, possibly on the ruins of an earlier temple. Damaged in the siege that brought Veii under Roman control early in the fourth century BC, it was leveled sometime later.

The pool, made of blocks of volcanic tufa plastered with clay and almost perfectly preserved, lies just north of the temple at the site's west end. Once fed by runoff from the mountainside that was channeled through a tunnel, the pool was probably used not for healing, as earlier scholars had thought, but for purification or initiation rites associated with Apollo's role as an oracle.

An outdoor sanctuary at the east end of the enclosure was also built with tufa blocks and featured a raised, rectangular altar and a pit where sacrifices were performed; the carbonized remains of these sacrifices were still evident at the time of the sanctuary's discovery. Nearby once stood a small structure filled with inscribed votive offerings dedicated to the goddess Minerva. Among them, excavators recovered statuettes of breasts and uteri, of women holding or feeding children, and of married couples, leading archaeologists to conclude that the worshipers who left them revered the divinity as the protector of procreation, birth, and childhood.

A new study of the site and its artifacts has led to a reassessment of the main temple's floor plan and to a fresh reconstruction of the temple itself *(page 130)*. Today, visitors can more easily imagine the building as it must have looked in its heyday, thanks to a scaffoldlike superstructure of thin iron rods that has been erected on the original foundation and adorned with models of the acroteria. The

Swaddled tightly and wearing an amulet, or bulla, around his neck, this fourth-century-BC votive figure of a baby was uncovered at Veii. Aristocratic Etruscan parents proudly bestowed such ornaments as the bulla upon their children as symbols of their patrician class.

new reconstruction assumes the shape of a square temple—not almost square, as Vitruvius had dictated—whose sides are each 60 feet long. (A previous reconstruction, completed around 1940, was based on what has since proved to be faulty archaeological evidence and resulted in a foundation that adhered strictly, if incorrectly, to Vitruvian proportions and specifications.)

A large quantity of painted terra-cotta fragments have been found at the site, and from these, scholars have been able to deduce the height of the original temple and its ornamentation. The most recent archaeological evidence also indicates that the original portico had only two columns, rather than the eight that were attributed to the "ideal" Etruscan temple. True to that Vitruvian ideal, however, this portico was backed by three cellae, an observation confirmed by the discovery of two kinds of clay paneling that would have been used on the door jambs—one on the jambs of the central cella and another, slightly smaller version on the jambs of the two side chambers.

The Portonaccio temple was surpassed in size and rivaled in splendor by a pair of temples at the port city of Pyrgi, the foundations of which were unearthed in 1957, in the course of the same dig that brought the Pyrgi plaques to light. Like the temple at Veii, the Pyrgi structures, designated Temple A and Temple B in their order of excavation, were embellished with painted terra-cotta facing and decorations, and their rooflines were studded with acroteria.

Temple A, the larger of the two, was constructed between 480 and 470 BC, and its floor plan matches that of the Vitruvian archetype: three cellae and a colon-

Hundreds of terra-cotta representations of wombs, left as votive gifts in the second century BC, fill an altar chamber at a temple site in Vulci dedicated to Uni, an Etruscan goddess associated with fertility and often identified with the Roman mother goddess, Juno. Body parts were popular offerings to the gods who monitored human health. To keep up with the demand for these items, terra-cotta ears, hands, and feet were mass produced in Etruria by means of stamps and molds.

The foundations of the Pyrgi temples, laid in the fifth century BC, were first unearthed in the 1950s, when deep plowing along the Tyrrhenian coastline revealed bits of tiles and terra cotta. Archaeologists intervened and excavated the site, producing the ground plan at right.

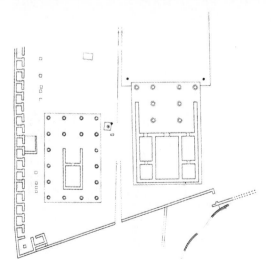

naded portico. The superstructure—built, like all Etruscan structures, of wood and unfired brick atop a stone podium—has not survived. But fragments of a large painted terra-cotta relief were found near one of the walls. Obviously handmade, not molded, it still bears the imprints of its artist's fingers, while its figures—approximately two-thirds life size—depict a scene from a famous Theban legend. Because of its theme and because it probably adorned the temple's pediment, a characteristic of Greek temples not found in similar Etruscan structures, the relief provides strong evidence of Greek influence in the Pyrgi area.

Further evidence is apparent in the architecture of Temple B, which dates to around 500 BC. Like the typical Greek temple, it features a single cella surrounded on all four sides by columns. It is this temple that, according to the Pyrgi plaques, the Etruscan king Thefarie Velianas dedicated to a Phoenician goddess. Indeed, Temple B's association with the deity has sparked speculation among some schol-

This terra-cotta relief once decorated the pediment of Temple A at Pyrgi. It shows a protagonist of a Greek myth, Tydeus, (foreground) devouring the brain of his rival, Melanippus, while Athena (far left) approaches and Zeus (center) *raises his arm to fight. Scholars painstakingly reassembled the work from surviving fragments found on site.*

TOMBS AND ROBBERS: THE VASE THAT PRODUCED AN ART–WORLD SCANDAL

As it happened, their fingerprints were all over one of the more sensational "finds" of recent years. At the center of the ensuing scandal was the Metropolitan Museum of Art's director, Thomas Hoving, who late in 1971 received word that an American antiquities dealer in Rome had just accepted a consignment with a "startling piece" that could be made available to the museum. This piece, which Hoving would later describe in a book about his career as the most "perfect work of art" he had ever encountered, was a calyx krater, an enormous Greek vase crafted around 510 BC *(opposite, below)*. Purportedly, it was owned by an Armenian coin dealer living in Beirut, who had inherited it unrestored, in pieces.

As director of the Metropolitan, Hoving was aware of the pitfalls of acquiring ancient art in an age when so much of it is smuggled onto the marketplace. Yet, given the chance to acquire what he called "the finest Greek vase there is," he authorized only the most cursory examination of the krater's pedigree in the months of negotiations that preceded the vase's purchase by the Metropolitan for one million dollars.

The *New York Times* began to question the provenance of the piece and deduced that the

The plunder of Etruria, begun under the Romans and accelerated in the 1700s with the onset of Etruscomania, continues to the present. Indeed, archaeologists estimate that some 85 percent of Etruscan tombs have been plundered over the centuries, despite numerous official attempts to stem the thievery, including one widely ignored law against the looting of ancient sites passed by the Romans themselves.

Among the more accomplished of modern-day thieves are the peasant farmers who, like the man above concealing his identity behind an Etruscan plaque, moonlight as *tombaroli,* or tomb robbers.

vase, rather than being—as the owner had claimed—in his family's hands since 1920, had actually been stolen in 1971 from a tomb in Cerveteri by tombaroli.

Theoretically, Italian law, which gives the state the right to everything antique recovered from Italian soil and imposes heavy fines on violators, should have kept the vase inside Italy. Theoretically, too, it would be more difficult today for a foreign museum to acquire Etruscan artifacts through so-called indirect means, thanks to stiffer penalties and stronger enforcement in the field. Nevertheless, for the tombaroli and their eager clients, life still goes on—and the vase sits handsomely restored in the Metropolitan.

ars that the Pyrgi sanctuary, and specifically a long, motel-like row of adjoining cells located to one side of Temple B, may have been the venue for ritual prostitution, a practice engaged in by the Greeks and Phoenicians that may have been intended as a way for worshipers to achieve communion with the divine. Archaeologists have uncovered inscriptions suggesting that the custom was followed at only one other site in Etruria: the port city Graviscae.

A restorer studies the snake-wielding Blue Demon, from the late-fifth- or early-fourth-century-BC tomb of the same name in Tarquinia. Though menacing in appearance, the Etruscan demons, both male and female, are not believed to have been seen as punishers of the dead, but as fearful companions to the dead on their journey to the underworld. They often guard the entrance to the tomb, perhaps to prevent the living from entering the home of the deceased.

The evolution of Etruria's religion and culture was reflected in its art as much as its architecture, and nowhere were those changes more evident than in the underground tombs. Some of these, in addition to housing the remains of the dead and the necessary accouterments for the good life in the hereafter *(pages 109-117)*, also functioned as art galleries, their walls adorned with colorful paintings whose style and content offer archaeologists a remarkably vivid glimpse of the Etruscans' way of life—and their way of death.

The paintings cover the period from the seventh to the first centuries BC and document the Etruscans' changing attitudes toward death and the afterlife. Until the end of the fifth century BC, of course, tomb paintings are generally celebratory, imbued with a *joie de vivre* that the Etruscans obviously believed would endure in the next world. But beginning in the fourth century BC, the artistic style and the mood of the paintings changed.

On the one hand, the murals show a greater mastery of technique on the part of their artists. Color, shading, and highlighting are used more effectively, and an understanding of perspective lends the works more depth and realism. But the paintings are somber, even sinister, and an air of foreboding has replaced the joy evident earlier. Moreover, death is portrayed not as a sumptuous and never-ending banquet, but as a mournful journey to a bleak netherworld bedeviled by demons and ghoulish deities. Charun, who as the Greek Charon was believed to ferry souls across the River Styx, is a fixture in these paintings, as are such thoroughly Etruscan creations as the winged, Fury-like Vanth and the monstrous Tuchulcha.

Color and detail add to the oppressive gloom of the paintings. The resident demons *(left)* are invariably a hideous shade of blue or green, and Charun, in particular, has the unmistakable blue-gray hue of decaying flesh. Symbolic of the role he was believed to play in dispatching those marked for death, he is often shown mallet in hand. Vanth, for her part, often carries a torch and sometimes bears an inscribed scroll, while the frightful Tuchulcha has the face of a vulture, the ears of a donkey, and a mass of writhing, open-jawed snakes for hair.

The tension between the old conception of the afterlife and the new is captured most tellingly on two adjoining walls in the Tomb of the Blue Demons, a rock-cut chamber discovered in 1986 under a modern highway in Tarquinia. On one wall, guests on couches enjoy food and drink and listen to the trill of a pipe at a traditional Etruscan banquet. On another are the demons that gave the tomb its name: One, painted blue, holds a coiled snake in each hand; another, black-winged and the very incarnation of evil, lunges forward, his teeth bared, his lips dripping blood. To their left are other figures, including that of a boy and a woman newly arrived in the land of the dead, having just disembarked from a reddish boat piloted by a paddle-wielding Charun.

The paintings owe their discovery to the construction of a new water main in 1985. Archaeological soundings along the proposed path of the pipeline revealed the entrances to 29 tombs, one of which was intriguing enough to warrant the use of the photographic probe invented in the late 1950s by Carlo Lerici. The ensuing excavations revealed that robbers had made off with the tomb's treasures and left behind little but the rock-fast wall paintings. Preliminary studies have since dated the tomb to a time in the late fifth or early fourth century BC, giving its mural the distinction of being the oldest such "demon" painting uncovered so far and the only one to show Charun in his traditional role as the ferryman of souls rather than as his mallet-bearing alter ego.

Scholars speculate that the new somber view of the afterlife reflects the influence of the Greek art of southern Italy, where scenes of the underworld were popular. The change in tomb art may also express the fears and anxieties that no doubt accompanied the centuries-long disintegration of Etruscan civilization. The downfall began at the end of the golden age of the city-states. Then, in the early part of the sixth century BC, the Etruscans were at the height of their power and even Rome was the domain of Etruscan kings. In fact, as Tarquinius Superbus, the ruler of Rome since 535 BC, busied himself with the construction of the Temple of Jupiter, he could hardly have imagined that his reign would mark the end of the Tarquin dynasty, which had been established less than a century earlier by Lucius Tarquinius Priscus. But fanned by royal arrogance, revolution blew in the wind, and in 509 BC, Superbus was expelled and the Roman Republic established.

The republic's uneasy birth was attended by increasing tension between Etruscans and Greeks, who were wreaking havoc with the trade that was so vital to the economic well-being of the Etruscan cities. Naval forces from the city of Caere successfully thwarted Greek attempts to colonize the island of Corsica early in the century, but in 524 BC, Caeretans and Etruscans from other city-states fought the Greeks again, this time with different results. Ancient accounts of the battle tell of an army of half a million Etruscans falling before a far smaller army of Greeks outside the

PAINTINGS TINGED WITH BLOOD

In 1857 the Italian archaeologist Alessandro François and his colleagues entered a fourth-century-BC Etruscan tomb they had just excavated in Vulci, Italy. Fascinated, they watched in the flickering torchlight as the walls, one by one, came into view. Adorning them were three sets of paintings, most of them well preserved and all carefully labeled.

One group consisted of mythological scenes, fairly violent in content. Of these, the largest illustrated an episode in the epic of the Trojan War, the *Iliad*, in which the Greek hero

Achilles sacrifices Trojan prisoners on the tomb of his friend Patroclus *(detail, below)*. Another set showed sixth-century-BC warriors of Vulci defeating Roman soldiers. The third included the earliest known full-length portrait done in Europe, of Vel Saties, the tomb's occupant, wearing a decorated mantle signaling his triumph in battle, probably against the Romans. The recurrence of the victory theme, in three different eras, points out the Etruscans' cyclical view of history.

In the segment reproduced here, Achilles is about to slit a prisoner's throat, attended by Patroclus's ghost *(right);* Vanth, a winged, female angel of death *(left);* and the demon Charun *(center)*, who lifts his hammer, perhaps to administer the *coup de grâce.*

This scene of slaughter with its religious overtones has been studied by American classicist Larissa Bonfante. She thinks the painting may reflect the Etruscan custom of sacrificing humans to honor the dead. Such bloodletting is known to have occurred as late as 356 BC, when, for example, the Etruscans offered up 307 captured Roman soldiers. The wall painting may have been commissioned in conjunction with just such a ritual killing—or in its stead. Whatever the case, sacrifice was to be perpetuated, says Bonfante, in the Etruscan-influenced Roman practice of gladiatorial games commemorating victories.

Greek colony of Cumae, south of Rome near Naples. Then, in 510 BC, another Greek colony, Croton, overran its neighbor—and Etruscan trading partner—Sybaris.

The Crotonian victory gave the Greeks control of the shipping lanes that passed through the Straits of Messina separating the toe of Italy from Sicily. Even more important, it set the stage for another, more decisive, encounter between Etruscans and Greeks from Syracuse, who had recently dealt a crushing blow to the Etruscans' ally, the Carthaginians. The collision came in 474 BC on the waters of the Tyrrhenian Sea off the coast of Cumae, and its outcome can be read in an inscription on a bronze Etruscan helmet unearthed in Greece in 1817, "Hiero, son of Deinomenes, and the Syracusans [dedicate] to Zeus the Etruscan spoils won at Cumae." The Etruscans' long-held links to the sea were severed.

The archaeological and historical evidence points to a downturn in the Etruscan economy in the wake of the Greek victory at Cumae and the subsequent expansion of Greek trade that came at the expense of the chastened Etruscans. Fewer luxury goods were imported during the fifth century BC, for example, and the quality of domestically produced bronzes and ceramics steadily declined. Few large-scale monuments were built, too, and no new public buildings. Even the dead had to make do with less, and some with nothing at all. Of those aristocrats lucky enough to find a final home in the great necropolises of Caere, Tarquinia, and Orvieto, most, to judge from the cheaper offerings and furnishings, were much more modestly outfitted for the afterlife than might otherwise have been expected; the less lucky never made it to the cemeteries at all. Indeed, archaeologists investigating the cemeteries have discovered that there were fewer burials in them than in earlier times.

Among the living, all that belt tightening only widened the gap between the haves and have-nots and in a few instances touched off social unrest at home. It also left the city-states of Etruria ill-prepared for the growing threat at their borders. Indeed, the peoples of the Samnite hills—ancient enemies of Rome who lived in central Italy, in what is today the region of Abruzzi—took advantage of the situation to force a wedge between the Etruscan heartland and its southern colonies in Campania. At the same time a youthful Rome was testing its strength by pouncing on allies of Veii, the Etruscan city closest to it, beginning with Fidenae in 426 BC. Then, two decades afterward, the Romans began a siege of Veii itself that would

A man battles his enemies with a plow on this terra-cotta urn from Chiusi. Similar scenes were commonly produced during the second century BC, a time of protracted social upheaval in the former Etruscan city-states.

bridge the end of the fifth century BC and the start of the fourth.

For most of the decade-long campaign, which tradition has likened to the Homeric siege of Troy, Veii's clifftop location and nearly impregnable city walls stood it in good stead. In the end, according to Livy, "she fell by a stratagem and not by assault," as the frustrated Romans finally recognized the futility of a frontal attack and instead tunneled under the city. Livy's testimony notwithstanding, no trace of such a shaft has been found, although it is possible that the Romans simply slithered into the city through the existing system of water channels. The surprise was total. Livy describes the scene as Veii was overrun: "A fearful din arose: yells of triumph, shrieks of terror, wailing of women, and the pitiful crying of children; in an instant of time the defenders were flung from the walls and the town gates opened; Roman troops came pouring through."

By the time Veii's enemies finally sheathed their swords in 396 BC, the city had been sacked, statues of its gods had been removed, its inhabitants slaughtered or hauled off into slavery, its territory annexed by its conquerors. Tragically, the other Etruscan cities had looked away as one of their own was gnawed off and swallowed by Rome, little suspecting, apparently, that they too could share Veii's dismal fate. The victorious Romans, however, would not go entirely unbloodied—but not at the hands of the Etruscans.

By some accounts, on the very day that Veii fell, the Gauls, who had for some time been infiltrating the Po Valley, pushed southward, overrunning Bologna and Marzabotto. Flush with victory, they crossed the Apennines around 390 BC and attacked Clusium. There, according to Livy, the locals were confronted by "strange men in thousands at the gates, men the likes of whom the townsfolk had never seen, outlandish warriors armed with strange weapons, who were already rumored to have scattered the Etruscan legions on both sides of the Po."

Although the people of Clusium certainly had their hands full, they actually faced only part of the Gallic force. The main body of the invaders made an end run and swept down on Rome. There, those Romans who could leave did so, including the priests and the vestal virgins, the maidens who kept watch over the sacred eternal fire of Vesta, the Roman goddess of the hearth. They took up an offer of asylum from the Etruscan city of Caere. The rest watched as the Gauls entered and torched everything but the capitol. Then, having come, seen, and conquered, the invaders accepted the tribute they were offered and left. For safeguarding the priests and vestal virgins, the Romans rewarded the residents of Caere with honorary Roman citizenship, then returned their attention to their budding confederation and to southern Etruria.

By the middle of the fourth century BC, several Etruscan cities—including Caere and especially Tarquinia—decided to attack. One by one, however, they were defeated, and one by one they became the subjects of Rome. Not until 311 BC did the remaining Etruscan cities join forces to take on the Romans at Sutri, a settlement near Tarquinia's boundary with Roman territory; repulsed once, they returned the following year and were soundly beaten. The Etruscans tried again in 295 BC, this time in league with their old enemies, the Gauls, as well as the Samnites, only to be decisively defeated at Sentinum, present-day Sassoferrato, roughly midway between Perugia and Ancona. According to the Greek historian Douris, the battle cost 100,000 lives. A last stand took place in 283 BC, when a coalition of Etruscans and Gauls was crushed near Lake Vadimo, located between Lake Bolsena and the Tiber River.

The effects of this struggle for power can be traced in an Etruscan tomb, albeit in inscriptions on urns rather than in paintings on walls. The tomb, carved into a hillside near Perugia, was discovered by accident in 1983 by a gardener who, in the course of pruning the fruit trees in his orchard, literally fell into good fortune when the ground gave way beneath him.

Archaeologists arrived at the site the following day, and excavations began immediately. Inside the perfectly preserved tomb, its door slab still in place, they found numerous artifacts, including 50 limestone urns containing the cremated remains of family members who had lived from the third to the first centuries BC. Most interesting to the researchers were the inscriptions in Etruscan on the urns, the oldest of which bore the name Cai Cutu. But on later urns, the first part of the name—a linguistic clue to the family's status as slaves—no longer appears; the Cutu family, it would appear, had won their freedom. More momentous changes were to come, however, and not just for the Cutu, but for their neighbors as well. Indeed, the latest inscriptions bear a telltale sign of increasing Roman influence: No longer in Etruscan, they are now written in Latin, and even the name Cutu has been Latinized to Cutius.

What happened in Perugia would occur throughout Etruria. By 280 BC, all of the Etruscan city-states had become subject-allies of the Roman Republic. Though they were barred from carrying on political relations with other states and their citizens now had to serve in the Roman army, various cities still enjoyed a degree of autonomy, and one of them, Volsinii, proved to be a thorn in the Romans' side. Four times during the fourth and third centuries BC it had warred against Rome—the last battle was in 280 BC—and four times it had humbly accepted a truce.

So in 265 BC, when the city's ruling families asked for help in quelling an internal revolt, Rome saw a chance to settle old scores once and for all. According to Johannes Zonoras, a 12th-century Byzantine historian, Rome put down the revolt, then leveled the city, thought to lie near Orvieto, and rebuilt it about nine miles to the southwest, on the shores of Lake Bolsena—a more vulnerable location where, presumably, the Volsiniians would think twice before daring to cross swords with the Romans again.

French archaeologists excavating near the modern town of Bolsena in 1946 found the remains of an ancient city that they identified as the Roman Volsinii. In addition to two private houses, one of which was owned by a man with the Latin name Laberius Gallus, the researchers uncovered baths, a forum, an amphitheater, and a theater. Yet the archaeologists also found traces of city walls that were built of large squared blocks years before the events described by Zonoras. Constructed sometime in the fourth century BC, they enclosed the part of the town that was later occupied by Roman Volsinii. This find has led some scholars to argue that the Roman and Etruscan towns shared city walls and that the removal of the Etruscan Volsinii never took place, though no one can say for sure.

What is certain is that after the Romans put down the revolt, they took as booty 2,000 bronze statues. The pieces were carried to the capital of the republic and worked into the decor of temples and public buildings. A Roman consul wrote that one of the monuments erected in Rome still bore the imprints of the feet and other traces of the bronze statues that had once adorned it. Since the old Volsinii had been the site of the sanctuary of the Etruscan god Voltumna, and thus served as the annual meeting place for the lucumones of the 12 Etruscan city-states, the removal of the statues served to underscore Rome's supremacy. It also marked the beginning of the plunder of Etruria, a process that became well established under the Romans, accelerated in the 18th century, and continues unabated to this day.

With the fate of Etruria tied to that of Rome, the Etruscans—fatalists that they were—seemed willing to bow to the inevitable. Faced with one last Gallic incursion south of the Apennines late in the third century BC, they sided with the Romans in dealing the invaders a decisive defeat. Likewise, during the Second Punic War, which Rome fought against the Carthaginians from 218 to 201 BC, they remained unswervingly loyal to their new masters, even though they might have taken advantage of Rome's preoccupation with the great

Known as the **Orator** *because of his noble stance, this bronze statue dating from around 100 BC is the only large-scale, late Etruscan statue that has survived intact. Originally cast in seven pieces by the lost-wax method, the piece strongly resembles Republican Roman statuary and could be mistaken for a Roman piece. However, scholars are able to identify its origins as Etruscan because the dedication, inscribed along the hem, is in the Etruscan language, not Latin.*

general Hannibal to stage their own rebellion. Upholding their end of the bargain, the Romans quickly and cruelly put down a revolt of Etruscan slaves in 196 BC.

The years that followed, according to the Italian archaeologist and historian Mario Torelli, are among the most obscure of all the obscure periods in Etruscan history. Yet the temper of the age is clear: one of economic hardship, especially in the south, followed in the early decades of the first century BC by what Torelli described as a "time of terror and general social and ethnic upheaval, marked by a serious breakdown of morale and psychological disorientation." Only under the rule of the triumvirate that succeeded Julius Caesar after his assassination in 44 BC would a modicum of economic and social stability return to Italy.

Later, as the Roman Empire muscled its way onto the world stage, many Etruscans must have felt that their unwavering belief in a fixed number of saecula and in preordained life cycles was about to be justified. But some scholars, including Torelli, see Etruscan fatalism as a self-fulfilling prophecy. "It was a collective suicide," he concluded. "Toward the end their priests would interpret such things as insect swarms as signs that the 'last Etruscan century' had arrived. At the end they just wanted to merge with the Roman world."

Yet in merging with that world, the Etruscans bequeathed a rich and living heritage to the Romans and, through them, to Western civilization as a whole. In the centuries since, some have imagined a mystery where none ever existed, wondering how a people who had contributed so much to the *koine*—the common culture of Italy that found its greatest expression in imperial Rome—could have disappeared from the cultural map of Europe so abruptly. What had become of the Etruscans, a people who had indeed filled the whole length of Italy with the fame of her name?

The answer can be found in a life-size bronze statue known as the *Orator*. Found near Cortona and dating to about 100 BC, it was sculpted by an Etruscan artist, and it depicts an actual Etruscan, one Aule Metele. His name is etched in Etruscan on the hem of his toga. His face, however, is a Roman face, his shoes Roman shoes, his stance the stance of any Roman senator addressing his peers. The Etruscans, he seems to say by his gesture and expression, had done what good Etruscans had always done. In the end they had simply accepted their fate; having found themselves in Rome, they had learned to do as the Romans do.

A HOMEGROWN GLORY

"In our time, that is in 1554, when trenches, fortifications and ramparts were being made at Arezzo, there was found a bronze sculpture . . . the Chimera." Thus wrote the Florentine artist Giorgio Vasari in his *Lives of the Artists (right)* about the emergence from Tuscan soil of a fourth-century-BC masterpiece—a four-foot-long, bronze mythological beast traditionally rendered as a lion with a snake tail and a goat's head sprouting from its back *(below)*. From the votive inscription on the right foreleg, the piece was recognized as Etruscan and whisked away to the Florentine palace of Cosimo de' Medici, the grand duke of Tuscany, in the heart of ancient Etruria. The exquisite artifacts surfacing from Etruscan tombs at this time fueled an awareness and pride in these early Italians amid the general Renaissance mania for the classical past. Cosimo's fascination helped initiate a process of rediscovery that has shaped art, architecture, interior design, and pottery right to the present day.

LE VITE
DE' PIV ECCELLENTI PITTORI,
SCVLTORI, E ARCHITETTORI

Scritte
DA M. GIORGIO VASARI PITTORE
ET ARCHITETTO ARETINO,
Di Nuovo dal Medesimo Riuiste
Et Ampliate
CON I RITRATTI LORO
Et con l'aggiunta delle Vite de'viui, & de'morti
Dall'anno 1550. insino al 1567.

Prima, e Seconda Parte.
Con le Tauole in ciascun Volume, Delle cose piu Notabili,
De' Ritratti, Delle Vite degli Artefici, Et de i
Luoghi doue sono l'opere loro.

CON LICENZA E PRIVILEGIO DI N. S. PIO V. ET
DEL DVCA DI FIORENZA E SIENA.

IN FIORENZA, Appresso i Giunti 1568.

INSPIRATION ROOTED IN THE PAST

Using tiny hammers and gold-smith's chisels, the brilliant and mercurial artist Benvenuto Cellini spent long evenings restoring tiny Etruscan statuettes in the grand duke's inner chambers. Cellini was only one of many Renaissance luminaries who studied and were inspired by the tomb paintings, sarcophagi, bronze mirrors, and sculptures of the Etruscans: Donatello, Michelangelo, Leonardo da Vinci, Brunelleschi, Alberti, Masaccio, Vasari, Sansovino, and Ghiberti all contributed to the Etruscan revival through their work and, in doing so, they were to influence artists and architects for centuries to come.

While most Renaissance mortuary sculpture places the pious dead flat on their backs with folded, prayerful arms, sculptor Andrea Sansovino's 1509 tomb of Cardinal Girolamo Basso della Rovere in Rome (right) reflects the influence of Etruscan sarcophagi. The painted fourth-century-BC, seven-foot-long example from Tarquinia below is typical, showing the occupant alive, lounging on his side.

9873

A Florentine treasure, Cellini's famed 10½-foot-tall bronze Perseus may well have been inspired by the Etruscan statuettes the artist was restoring at the time. The stance, nudity, sickle-shaped sword, and winged cap are echoed at right in a 350-BC bronze Perseus and above in the Renaissance drawing of an Etruscan bronze mirror depicting Odysseus threatening to decapitate Circe.

THE VIGOROUS ETRUSCAN ORDER

Although few of Etruria's structures survive, aspects of its bold architecture do. With a smooth column and rounded capital *(right)*, the Etruscan Doric column has become a builder's staple, from villas in the Tuscan hills to late-20th-century homes in the United States. Distinct from its fluted, Greek Doric sister, the Tuscan order was originally described by the Roman architect Vitruvius. Of all the Renaissance architects who drew upon Vetruvius's treatise, Andrea Palladio, in a vital reinterpretation of antiquity, had the most profound impact. Developing a graceful style of his own, he made use of this simple pillar in the elegantly distinctive houses that bear the name Palladian to this day.

The Etruscan column can be seen in this sixth-century-BC tomb at Cerveteri with mock-timbered ceiling. The order was sketched (below) *by Giorgio*

Vasari in his plans for the colonnaded Uffizi—the grand duke's Florentine offices that were constructed in 1560 and are today a museum.

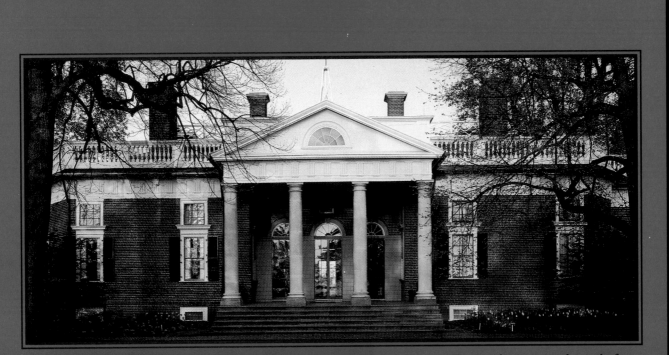

*Tuscan columns grace the porch of
Thomas Jefferson's Monticello. An ar-
dent reader of Palladio's four-volume
architectural treatise, Jefferson was the
first to design and build a Palladian
villa in America.*

*Acroteria—or statues borne by pedestals
on the corners and peak of a pediment—constitute another quintessen-
tially Etruscan temple feature used by
Palladio and seen here in his 16th-
century Church of San Giorgio Mag-
giore in Venice.*

REINVENTING THE ARTS OF ETRURIA

The 18th century ushered in the era of the grand tour, when members of European polite society traipsed through the ruins of ancient Greece and Italy, admiring and collecting antiquities. One such famed antiquarian was Sir William Hamilton, who was the British consul to the kingdom of Naples during the latter half of the 18th century. His collection and 1766 catalog describing Etrurian vases proved a vital stimulus to artistic tastes of the day. Studied by designers, decorators, and patrons alike, both helped shape the growth of neoclassicism. Josiah Wedgwood, the famed English potter, was so inspired by Hamilton's catalog that he named his factory Etruria—though, in truth, most of the vases Hamilton brought back turned out to be Greek.

In this 1798 watercolor by an anonymous Neapolitan, Sir William Hamilton (the tall figure at the far right) *displays his famed collection of Greek vases to an appreciative audience of travelers. Though his first collection made its way safely to the British Museum, the second was shipwrecked off the coast of England in 1798—only sherds remain of this lost glory.*

In this 19th-century engraving, Wedgwood is seated in the throwing room of his ceramic factory in Staffordshire, England. To commemorate the 1769 opening, he threw the first six vases himself, copying the red-figure designs from vessels in Hamilton's catalog, as in the example seen below.

JUNE XIII .M.DCC.LXIX. of the first Days Productions at Etruria in Staffordshire by Wedgwood and Bentley

On the reverse side (right) of the Wedgwood vase above, a Latin inscription reads, "The Arts of Etruria Are Reborn," reflecting the false but widespread belief that the Greek-style vases found there were Etruscan. Wedgwood also copied real Etruscan bucchero ware as well as the almost foot-high, fourth-century-BC bronze vase in the shape of a young man's head seen at left.

A TASTE FOR ETRUSCAN STYLE

"In short, I am antique Mad," confessed Robert Adam, another "grand tourist" and young English architect whose four-year study of ancient Italian ruins impelled him to create his own distinctive decorative mode in architecture, interior design, and furniture. Known at first as "the Etruscan style," this early phase of neoclassicism was an eclectic and inventive amalgam of ancient Etruscan, Roman, Greek, and Egyptian motifs. Its name reflected the patriotic Italian trend of attributing to the Etruscans not only the Greek-style vases, but also various Greek achievements in architecture, science, and philosophy.

Two Etruscans have a tête-à-tête on Etruscan stools in this famed sixth-century-BC, painted terra-cotta plaque from Cerveteri. Later adopted by Roman magistrates as a symbol of dignity, such folding seats were again popularized during the Empire period in France. The gilded stool below—still bearing its original upholstery—was made in 1822.

"It is called Etruscan and painted all over like Wedgwood's ware" was one critic's 1778 reaction to Adam's design of the Etruscan Room at Osterley Park (right). Many motifs, such as the garlands and sphinxes, were inspired by artist-archaeologist Giovanni Battista Piranesi's 1769 book on interior design (below), which included Etruscan, Greek, and Roman designs.

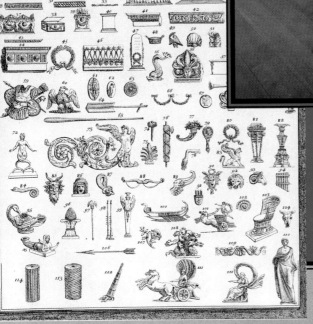

THE OLD REINTERPRETED

In Italy, Etruscomania never really died. "For Italians," says artist Arnaldo Pomodoro, "the Etruscans are in our roots." Sculptor Marino Marini added to that sentiment when he said, "We live among the monuments of the past. I, for instance, was born in Tuscany, where the rediscovery in the last 50 years of Etruscan art has been something of great importance in contemporary local life." Not surprisingly, the work of Pomodoro, Marini, and fellow artist Alberto Giacometti is filled with allusions to Etruscan tomb paintings, sculpture, and necropolises.

The design, texture, and colors of Marini's 1942 terracotta Cavaliere (left) echo the Etruscan wall painting above from the sixth-century-BC Tomb of the Bulls at Tarquinia. "I like going to the source of things," he wrote. "I am interested in a civilization at its beginning."

Etruscologists have remarked on the elongated proportions and uncanny resemblance between sculptor Alberto Giacometti's 1948, six-foot-tall bronze, "Standing Woman" (left) and the third-century-BC, two-foot-tall Etruscan bronze of a young boy (far left). Such expressiveness became a hallmark of Giacometti's work.

Reminiscent of Etruscan necropolises, Pomodoro's 1974 cemetery design was seen by the artist as "a crack in the hillside, opening to the sky." Urbino became embroiled in a fierce community debate over its paganism, and this "neo-Etruscan" work was never built.

ETRURIA'S INDELIBLE MARK ON HISTORY

Dwelling between the Arno and Tiber Rivers in west central Italy during the first millennium BC, the Etruscans rose swiftly to prominence in the ancient world, their mineral wealth a magnet for eager traders from other lands. Foremost among these merchants were the Greeks, who influenced the political, cultural, and artistic direction of Etruria, a loose confederation of independent city-states. The Etruscans, in turn, shaped others as they expanded their territory north and south and established a dynasty that ruled Rome for a hundred years.

Etruscan history is divided into a proto-Etruscan era (the Villanovan, named for the estate where its artifacts were first identified) and four later periods—Orientalizing, Archaic, Classical, and Hellenistic—based on phases of Greek history. These latter divisions are not strictly appropriate to the Etruscans but are generally used by scholars.

Etruria vanished almost as quickly as it had appeared. The Romans, once ruled by Etruscans, conquered the Etruscan city-states one by one, and by the beginning of the third century BC what could be called an independent Etruria no longer existed. Later, the Etruscans' language fell into disuse, and their written works ceased to be copied. But a part of Etruria survives, in the histories of Greeks and Romans, in evocative pieces of Etruscan artwork, and in the lasting imprint the Etruscans left on Western civilization.

VILLANOVAN PERIOD 1000-700 BC

IMPASTO CINERARY URN

The Iron Age people of the Villanovan period, the proto-Etruscans, lived in small villages of wattle-and-daub huts, often clustered on hills and other easily defensible positions. Regional differences existed, but the culture was fairly homogeneous and egalitarian in nature. Burials, for instance, showed no great distinction based on social rank or wealth. The dead were usually cremated, their ashes placed in an impasto (unrefined clay) or terra-cotta urn—sometimes shaped as a hut (*above*)—which was buried in a circular pit.

Change arrived early in the eighth century BC. Greek traders from the Aegean island of Euboea were drawn to the western side of Italy by its vast mineral wealth. The Euboeans founded a trading colony, Pithecusae, on the Italian island of Ischia. In the next few decades, so many Greek colonies were established on the coasts of southern Italy and Sicily that later writers dubbed the area Magna Graecia (Great Greece).

Trade from the east brought new ideas as well as material wealth. A new aristocratic class arose. Crafts became specialized. And the villages began to consolidate into larger towns, which would become the cities of Etruria.

ORIENTALIZING PERIOD 700-600 BC

BUCCHERO PYXIS

Made rich by trade, the Etruscan cities flourished in the seventh century. Despite a shared culture and history, however, they composed not a country but a loose confederation of city-states, each ruled by its own government. Their inhabitants were master seafarers, who ruled the Tyrrhenian Sea and protected Etruscan shores and interests.

Etruscan minerals, so scarce elsewhere in the Mediterranean, were traded for luxury goods from Egypt, the Levant, Syria, Asia Minor, and Greece. Local art assumed Oriental, or Middle Eastern, motifs (many borrowed from the Greeks), but skilled Etruscan artisans were never mere imitators. They developed a high-quality black pottery called bucchero, for instance, and used it to make objects traditionally done in metal (*above*).

The Greeks brought the alphabet to Etruria before 700 BC. By the end of the seventh century, Etruscans had adopted Greek mythology and were fortifying their cities with cut stone walls as the Greeks did. Aristocratic banqueting, hunting, and ceremonial games were based on Greek models as well.

Meanwhile, the Etruscans' influence began to spread south, near the Greek colonies. In 616 BC, the Etruscan Lucius Tarquinius Priscus became ruler of Rome.

ARCHAIC PERIOD
600-480 BC

TARQUINIA WALL PAINTING

CLASSICAL PERIOD
480-300 BC

TERRA-COTTA HORSES

HELLENISTIC PERIOD
300-89 BC

BRONZE HEAD OF A BOY

The Etruscans reached their zenith in the sixth century BC, expanding north across the Apennines. The Etruscan rulers of the Tarquin dynasty transformed Rome into an urban center, building monumental structures, paving the Forum, and installing a sewer system.

Etruscan art, often inspired by Greek work, thrived, particularly in architecture, sculpture, and painting. Colorful and lively painted figures (*above*) filled the walls of monumental tombs.

Outside the art world, the Etruscans and Greeks battled for supremacy. Etruscans allied themselves with the Carthaginians to protect against the threat of Greek expansion. When Greeks from Phocaea settled on the island of Corsica, the allies were undoubtedly alarmed. Around 535 BC they fought a fierce naval battle with the Phocaeans, who won a narrow victory. The Phocaeans lost so many ships, however, that they were forced to abandon the colony. A decade later, a large Etruscan army near the Greek colony of Cumae, in Campania, fell to a much smaller Greek force.

In 509 BC the Tarquin dynasty came to an end when the people of Rome threw out Lucius Tarquinius Superbus, establishing a republic and changing forever the city-states' relationship to Rome.

Enemies threatened the Etruscans at every turn. Near Cumae, in 474 BC, Etruscans lost a sea battle to a Greek fleet from Syracuse. An emboldened Syracusan fleet then raided Etruscan sites on Elba and Corsica. In the north, the Gauls continued to attack Etruscans in the Po Valley, as they had since the previous century. Rome and the city-state of Veii began an intermittent conflict around 485 that would not be resolved until 396 BC, when Veii fell. In Campania, a force including Samnite tribes from central Italy attacked the now-isolated Etruscan colonies, capturing Capua in 423 BC.

Embattled on all sides, trade disrupted, southern Etruscan cities experienced a recession. Artisanship declined. Fortunately, the fourth century BC brought an economic and artistic revival. Greek style again influenced Etruscan art, as evidenced above by classical horses from Tarquinia.

The battles, however, continued. The Gauls moved south across the Apennines. From 358 to 351 BC, Tarquinia fought almost continuously with Rome, until the Etruscans were forced to sue for peace. Around 311 BC, the Etruscan city-states did what they had rarely done before: They united to fight an enemy. They laid siege to a Roman settlement, Sutri, but had to flee north when defeated.

Roman armies marched at will across Italy by the third century BC. Still defiant, some Etruscans united with the Samnites and Umbrians of central Italy and the Gauls on the other side of the Alps to challenge Rome. The republic crushed the combined army at Sentinum, in Umbria, in 295 BC. A decade later, Etruscans and Gauls battled Rome near Lake Vadimo, only to fall again to Roman might. By 280 the Etruscan city-states had become subject-allies of the Roman Republic, even supporting Rome when it waged war against the Carthaginians and the Gauls at the end of the century.

Greek Hellenistic artistic styles, including sculpture, could be found in Etruria around 300 BC (*above*). In this period and soon after, however, Etruscan art converged with Roman.

The continual wars and economic hardships created social problems, erupting in Volsinii around 265 BC as a struggle between serfs and aristocrats. Rome razed the city. The Romans also quickly suppressed an Etruscan slave uprising in 196 BC. In 89 BC, Rome conferred citizenship on the Etruscans, one of the final steps taken toward their complete Romanization.

ACKNOWLEDGMENTS

The editors wish to thank the following individuals and institutions for their valuable assistance in the preparation of this volume:

Bernard Andreae, Istituto Archeologico Germanico, Rome; Gaspare Baggieri, Servizio Tecnico per le Ricerche Antropologiche, Ministero per i Beni Culturali, Rome; Susan Baldwin, University of Evansville, Evansville, Indiana; Claudio Bettini, Soprintendenza Archeologica per l'Etruria Meridionale, Rome; Horst Blanck, Istituto Archeologico Germanico, Rome; Francesca Boitani, Soprintendenza Archeologica per l'Etruria Meridionale, Rome; Mensun Bound, MARE, University of Oxford, England; Umberto Bovoni, Volterra; Luigi Capasso, Servizio Tecnico per le Ricerche Antropologiche, Ministero per i Beni Culturali, Rome; Giorgio Caponetti, Tuscania; Maria Cataldi, Soprintendenza Archeologica per l'Etruria Meridionale, Rome; Giovanni Colonna, Rome; Giuliano De Marinis, Soprintendenza Archeologica della Toscana, Florence; Anna-Maria Esposito, Soprintendenza Archeologica della Toscana, Florence; Alberto Gargiuli, Tuscania; Gino Vinicio Gentili, Bologna; Cristiana Morigi Govi, Museo Civico Archeologico, Bologna; Renzo Giachetti, Soprintendenza Archeologica della Toscana, Florence; Paola Zamarchi Grassi, Soprintendenza Archeologica della Toscana, Florence; Pietro Giovanni Guzzo, Soprintendenza Archeologica dell'Emilia-Romagna, Bologna; Richard Hodges, British School at Rome, Rome; Jean-René Jannot, Nantes; Heidi Klein, Bildarchiv Preussischer Kulturbesitz, Berlin; Gioia Meconcelli, Museo Civico Archeologico, Bologna; I. Mirnik, Archaeological Museum, Zagreb, Croatia; Maria Montembault, Département des Antiquités Grecques et Romaines, Musé du Louvre, Paris; Giovanni Morigi, Bologna; Francesco Nicosia, Soprintendenza Archeologica della Toscana, Florence; Carl Nylander, Istituto Svedese di Studi Classici, Rome; Licia Palmieri, Soprintendenza Archeologica dell'Emilia-Romagna, Bologna; Tom B. Rasmussen, University of Manchester, England; A. Rendic'-Miocevic', Archaeological Museum, Zagreb, Croatia; David Ridgway, University of Edinburgh, Scotland; Sergio Sani, Marzabotto; Giovanni Scichilone, Soprintendenza Archeologica per l'Etruria Meridionale, Rome; Friedrich Wilhelm von Hase, Röisch-Germanisches Zentralmuseum, Mainz.

PICTURE CREDITS

The sources for the illustrations that appear in this volume are listed below. Credits from left to right are separated by semicolons, credits from top to bottom are separated by dashes.

Photographs supplied by regional superintendencies are by kind concession of the Ministry of Culture and Environment, Rome, copyright reserved. Cover: Scala, Florence. Background from *Civiltà degli Etruschi* by Electra editrice, Milan, 1985. End Paper: Art by Paul Breeden. 6, 7: © O. Louis Mazzatenta, National Geographic Society. 8: Mario Carrieri, Milan. 10: Soprintendenza Archeologica dell'Emilia-Romagna, Bologna; Museo Civico Archeologico, Bologna. 11: Museo Civico Archeologico, Bologna. 12: Giovanni Morigi, Bologna. 13: Giovanni Morigi, Bologna; Museo Civico Archeologico, Bologna—Gianni Dagli Orti, Paris. 14, 15: Mario Carrieri, Milan. 16, 17: Scala, Florence. 18: Giovanni Lattanzi, Giulianova/in the Laboratorio di Restauro of the Florence "Soprintendenza Archeologica." 21: Anderson/Fratelli Alinari, Florence. 23: The Metropolitan Museum of Art, Fletcher Fund, 1924 (24.97.21ab). 25: Fototeca Ufficio Beni A.A.A.A.S., Regione Umbria/Archiva Alinari, Florence. 26: Professor Giovanni Colonna, Rome. 27: Scala, Florence. 28: Scala, Florence; C. M. Dixon, Canterbury, Kent; Nimatallah/Ricciarini, Milan. 29: Scala, Florence; Marcello Bellisario, Rome; Scala, Florence. 30: Museo Civico Archeologico, Bologna; from reconstructions of Late Bronze Age/Iron Age structures by Cozza and Davico, from "Huts in the Central Tyrrhenian area of Italy during the protohistoric age." In *Papers in Italian Archaeology IV, vol. 3, Patterns in Protohistory*, edited by Malone, C.A.T., and Stoddart, S.K.F. British Archaeological Reports, Oxford, 175-202 (B.A.R. International Series 245). 32: Soprintendenza Archeologica della Toscana, Florence. 33: Nimatallah/Ricciarini, Milan. 35: Soprintendenza Archeologica delle Provincie di Napoli e Caserta, Naples. 37-39: Scala, Florence. 40, 41: Scala, Florence; Bildarchiv Claus Hansmann/Munich. 42, 43: Scala, Florence; Takashi Okamur, Rome. 44: The Toledo Museum of Art, Ohio/Gift of Edward Drummond Libbey/photo by Tim Thayer (1982.134). 46, 47: Dr. Mensun Bound, MARE, Oxford. 48, 49: Araldo De Luca, Rome. 50: Mauro Pucciarelli, Rome. 51: Scala, Florence. 52: Photo R.M.N., Paris. 53: From *Gli Etruschi, Cinque Miti da Sfatare* by Giampiero Pianu/Armando Curcio Editore, Rome, 1985—Scala, Florence. 54: Art by Angela Johnson. 55, 57: Scala, Florence. 58, 59: Nimatallah/Ricciarini, Milan—Scala, Florence. 60: © The British Museum, London. 62: Courtesy of Peggy White, Bolsover, Derbyshire, England. 63: From *The Cities and Cemeteries of Etruria* by George Dennis, published by John Murray, 1883; From *Dennis of Etruria* by Dennis Rhodes, Cecil Woolf Publishers, London, 1973. 64: Giovanni Lattanzi, Giulianova. 65:

Antonio Martinelli. 66: Gianni Dagli Orti, Paris—From *The Etruscans in the Museums of Rome* by Giovanna Sorrentino, Rome. 67: Pubbliaerfoto, Milan. 68: Crown copyright reserved/Air Photo Library, Keele University, Staffordshire, England. 69: Archivio Federico Patellani, Milan—Fondazione Lerici, Rome. 71: Scala, Florence. Background Dr. Erik O. Nielsen. 72, 73: Dr. Erik O. Nielsen (3)—G. Soderberg after D. Peck, art by Angela Johnson. Background Dr. Erik O. Nielsen. 74-81: Dr. Erik O. Nielsen. 82: Sergio Sani, Marzabotto. 85, 86: © The British Museum, London. 87: Drawing by Sue Bird, © The British Museum, London. 88, 89: Istituto Archeologico Germanico, Rome. 92: Nancy T. de Grummond. 94: Photo R.M.N., Paris. 95: Araldo De Luca/ Musei Vaticani, Rome. 97: Giovanni Lattanzi, Giulianova, courtesy Soprintendenza Archeologica per l'Etruria Meridionale, Rome. 99: Luigi Capasso, Servizio Tecnico per le Ricerche Antropologiche e Paleopatologiche, Chieti—Giovanni Lattanzi, Giulianova, courtesy Soprintendenza Archeologica per l'Etruria Meridionale, Rome. 100, 101: Giraudon, Lauros-Giraudon, Paris. 102: Jan Mark/Nordiska Museet, Stockholm. 103: AP/Wide World Photos; C. E. Ostenberg/Nordiska Museet, Stockholm—Istituto Svedese di Studi Clas-

sici, Rome; Börje Blomé, Stockholm. 104, 105: Scala, Florence. 106, 107: Museo Archeologico Nazionale, Ferrara. 109: Nimatallah/Ricciarini, Milan. 110, 111: Gianni Dagli Orti, Paris. 112, 113: Scala, Florence. 114: © Pierre Boulat/Woodfin Camp and Associates—Achille Bianchi/Franco Sperandei, Rome. 115: Courtesy Museum of Fine Arts, Boston. 116: Scala, Florence. 117: Scala, Florence—Nimatallah/Ricciarini, Milan. 118: Gianni Dagli Orti, Paris. 120, 121: Soprintendenza Archeologica della Toscana, Florence. 122: Scala, Florence. 123: Gianni Dagli Orti, Paris. 124: Bildarchiv Claus Hansmann/Munich. 125: Mario Carrieri, Milan. 126: Archivio I.G.D.A., Milan. 127: © O. Louis Mazzatenta, National Geographic Society. 129: © The British Museum, London. 130: Achille Bianchi/Franco Sperandei, Rome. 131: Bibliothéque Doucet, Paris/from *Giulio Quirino Giglioli: Arte Etrusca*. 132: Gianni Dagli Orti, Paris. 133: © O. Louis Mazzatenta, National Geographic Society. 134: Pubbliaerfoto, Milan—Professor Giovanni Colonna, Rome. 135: Scala, Florence. 136: © O. Louis Mazzatenta, National Geographic Society. 137: Giovanni Lattanzi, Giulianova—The Metropolitan Museum of Art, Purchase, Bequest of Joseph H. Durkee, Gift of Darius Ogden Mills and Gift of C. Ruxton Love, 1972. 138:

© O. Louis Mazzatenta, National Geographic Society. 140: David Lees, Florence. 142: Scala, Florence. 145: Nimatallah/Ricciarini, Milan. 147: © The British Library, London—Nimatallah/Ricciarini, Milan. 148: Alinari, Florence—Gianni Dagli Orti, Paris. 149: Scala/Art Resource; Staatsbibliothek zu Berlin Preussischer Kulturbesitz, Handschriftenabteilung—Museum für Kunst und Gewerbe, Hamburg, Inv 1929.22. 150: From *Cerveteri, Istituto Geografico De Agostini, Novara*, 1977, photo by Gianni Dagli Orti—Gabinetto dei Disegni e Stampe, Galleria degli Uffizi, Florence. 151: © Michael Freeman, London—Scala, Florence. 152: Stephen Natanson, courtesy of Ubaldo Carboni, Rome; Giraudon, Paris/courtesy Musée du Louvre. 153: From *The Life of Josiah Wedgwood* by Eliza Meteyard, London, 1865—The Trustees of the Wedgwood Museum, Barlaston, Staffordshire, England (2). 154: C. M. Dixon, Canterbury, Kent, England/Louvre, Paris—photo R.M.N. / Blot, Lewandowski. 155: Alberto Bertoldi/Gruppo Editoriale Fabbri, Milan—Bibliothèque Nationale de France. 156: Scala, Florence—Photo by David Finn. 157: Scala, Florence; Alberto Giacometti Foundation, Kunsthaus Zürich; painting by Arnaldo Pomodoro, Milan. 158-159: Art by Paul Breeden.

BIBLIOGRAPHY

Ackerman, James S. *Palladio*. London: Penguin Books, 1966.

Acton, Harold. *Three Extraordinary Ambassadors*. London: Thames and Hudson, 1983.

Alberto Giacometti: A Retrospective Exhibition. New York: The Solomon R. Guggenheim Museum, 1974.

The Autobiography of Benvenuto Cellini. Translated by J. Addington Symonds. Roslyn, N.Y.: Black's Readers Service, 1927.

Barker, Graeme, Annie Grant, and Tom Rasmussen. "Approaches to the Etruscan Landscape: The Develop-

ment of the Tuscania Survey." In *Case Studies in European Prehistory*, edited by Peter Bogucki. Boca Raton: CRC Press, 1993.

Bishop, Robert, and Patricia Coblentz. *Furniture 1: Prehistoric through Rococo*. Washington, D.C.: Cooper-Hewitt Museum of The Smithsonian Institution, 1979.

Boardman, John. *The Greeks Overseas: Their Early Colonies and Trade*. London: Thames and Hudson, 1980.

Boase, T. S. R. *Giorgio Vasari: The Man and the Book*. Princeton: Princeton University Press, 1979.

Boëthius, Alex, et al. *Etruscan Culture: Land and People*. Translated by Nils G. Sahlin. New York: Columbia University Press, 1962.

Boitani, Francesca, Maria Cataldi, and Marinella Pasquinucci. *Etruscan Cities*. New York: G.P. Putnam's, 1975.

Bonfante, Giuliano, and Larissa Bonfante. *The Etruscan Language*. New York: New York University Press, 1983.

Bonfante, Larissa:
Etruscan (Reading the Past series). London: British Museum Publica-

tions, 1990.

Etruscan Dress. Baltimore: The Johns Hopkins University Press, 1975.

"In Search of the Truth about Etruscan Women." In *Discovery of Lost Worlds,* edited by Joseph J. Thorndike, Jr. New York: American Heritage, 1979.

Out of Etruria: Etruscan Influence North and South. Oxford: B.A.R. International Series, 1981.

Bonfante, Larissa (ed.). *Etruscan Life and Afterlife.* Detroit: Wayne State University Press, 1986.

Bradford, John. *Ancient Landscapes: Studies in Field Archaeology.* London: G. Bell, 1957.

Bremner, M. D. K. *The Story of Dentistry: From the Dawn of Civilization to the Present.* London: Henry Kimpton's Medical House, 1946.

Bulfinch, Thomas. *Myths of Greece and Rome.* New York: Viking Penguin, 1979.

Buranelli, Francesco. *The Etruscans: Legacy of a Lost Civilization from the Vatican Museums.* Translated by Nancy Thomson de Grummond. Memphis: Wonders, The Memphis International Cultural Series, 1992.

Colonna, Giovanni. *Santuari d'Etruria.* Milan: Electa, 1985.

Crea, Benedetta Origo (ed.): *Etruria Unveiled:The Drawings of Samuel James Ainsley in the British Museum.* Rome: Edizioni dell'Elefante, 1984.

Cristofani, Mauro. *The Etruscans: A New Investigation.* London: Orbis, 1979.

Cristofani, Mauro (ed.). *Urne Volterrane.* Forence: Centro, 1975.

Dal Maso, Leonardo B., and Roberto Vighi (eds.). *Southern Etruria.* Translated by Michael Hollingworth. Florence: Bonechi-Edizioni, 1975.

de Grummond, Nancy Thomson (ed.): *A Dictionary of the History of Classical Archaeology.* Westport, Conn.: Greenwood Press, in press.

A Guide to Etruscan Mirrors. Tallahassee: Archaeological News, 1982.

Dennis, George. *The Cities and Cemeteries of Etruria.* London: John Murray, 1883.

DePuma, Richard Daniel, and Jocelyn Penny Small (eds.). *Murlo and the Etruscans: Art and Society in Ancient*

Etruria. Madison: The University of Wisconsin Press, 1994.

Diodorus of Sicily. Edited by T. E. Page, translated by C. H. Oldfather. Cambridge: Harvard University Press, 1939.

Edlund-Berry, Ingrid E. M. *The Seated and Standing Statue Akroteria from Poggio Civitate (Murlo).* Rome: Giorgio Bretschneider Editore, 1992.

Encyclopedia of World Art. New York: McGraw-Hill, 1959.

Falchi, Isidoro. *Vetulonia e la sua Necropoli Antichissima.* Florence: Le Monnier, 1891.

Fraser, Douglas, Howard Hibbard, and Milton J. Lewine (eds.). *Essays in the History of Architecture Presented to Rudolf Wittkower.* Bristol, England: Phaidon Press, 1967.

Gerhard, Eduard. *Etruskische Spiegel* (Vol. 4). New York: Walter De Gruyter, 1974.

Giacometti, Alberto. *Alberto Giacometti.* New York: Doubleday, 1965.

Gloag, John. *A Social History of Furniture Design from 1300 BC to AD 1960.* New York: Crown Books, 1966.

Govi, Cristiana Morigi, and Guiseppe Sassatelli (eds.). *Dalla Stanza delle Antichità al Museo Civico, Storia della Formazione del Museo Civil Archeologico di Bologna.* Bologna, 1984.

Grant, Michael. *The Etruscans.* New York: Charles Scribner's Sons, 1980.

Gray, Hamilton Mrs. *Tour to the Sepulchres of Etruria in 1839.* London: J. Hatchard, 1841.

Gray, John Hamilton. *Autobiography of a Scotch Country Gentleman.* Printed for Private Circulation, 1868.

Guerini, Vincenzo. *A History of Dentistry from the Most Ancient Times until the End of the Eighteenth Century.* Amsterdam: Liberac N.V., 1967.

Guida alla Citta' Etrusca e al Museo di Marzabotto. Bologna: Edizioni Alfa, 1982.

Guinness, Desmond, and Julius Trousdale Sadler. *Palladio: A Western Progress.* New York: The Viking Press, 1976.

Hamblin, Dora Jane. *Pots and Robbers.* New York: Simon and Schuster, 1970.

Hamblin, Dora Jane, and the Editors of Time-Life Books. *The Etruscans* (The Emergence of Man series).

New York: Time-Life Books, 1975.

Hawley, Henry. *Neo-Classicism: Style and Motif.* New York: Harry N. Abrams, 1964.

Haynes, Sybille. *Etruscan Bronzes.* New York: Harper & Row, 1985.

Hencken, Hugh O'Neill. *Tarquinia, Villanovans and Early Etruscans* (Vol. 1). Cambridge, Mass.: The Peabody Museum, 1968.

Hunter, Sam:
Arnaldo Pomodoro. New York: Abbeville Press, 1982.
Marino Marini: The Sculpture. Edited by Adele Westbrook. New York: Harry N. Abrams, 1993.

Jones, Mark (ed.). *Fake? The Art of Deception.* Berkeley: University of California Press, 1990.

Kelly, Alison. *The Story of Wedgwood.* London: Faber & Faber, 1975.

Kinsey, Joni, et al. *The Spirit of Antiquity.* St. Louis: Washington University Gallery of Art, 1984.

Kubly, Herbert, and the Editors of LIFE. *Italy* (Life World Library). New York: Time Incorporated, 1964.

Lapaire, Claude, and Jacques Chamay (eds.). *L'Art des Peuples Italiques: 3000A 300 Avant J.-C.* Rome: Electa Napoli, 1993.

Lawrence, D. *Etruscan Places.* London: The Folio Society, 1972.

Lerici, Carlo Maurilio. *A Great Adventure of Italian Archaeology.* Lerici Editori, 1966.

Les Etrusques et L'Europe. Paris: Editions de la Réunion des Musées Nationaux, 1992.

Livy. (Vols. 1 and 3). Translated by B. O. Foster. London: William Heinemann, 1924.

Lufkin, Arthur Ward. *A History of Dentistry.* Philadelphia: Lea & Febiger, 1948.

Macaulay, Thomas Babington. *Lays of Ancient Rome and Miscellaneous Essays and Poems.* London: J.M. Dent, 1968.

MacKendrick, Paul. *The Mute Stones Speak: The Story of Archaeology in Italy.* New York: W.W. Norton, 1983.

Macnamara, Ellen:
The Etruscans. London: The Trustees of the British Museum by British Museum Publications, 1990.
Everyday Life of the Etruscans. New York: Dorset Press, 1973.

McKay, Alexander G. *Vitruvius, Archi-*

tect and Engineer: Buildings and Building Techniques in Augustan Rome. London: Macmillan Education, 1978.

Momigliano, Arnaldo. *Studies in Historiography* (History and Historiography series). New York: Garland Publishing, 1985.

Morris, Roland. *HMS Colossus: The Story of the Salvage of the Hamilton Treasures.* London: Hutchinson, 1979.

Nestler, Gerhard, and Edilberto Formigli. *Etruskische Granulation.* Siena, Italy: Nuova Immagine Editrice, 1993.

Nickerson, David. *English Furniture of the Eighteenth Century.* New York: G.P. Putnam's Sons, 1963.

Le Origini della Chirurgia Italiana. Rome: Ministero per i Beni Culturali e Ambientali Servizio Tecnico per le Ricerche Antropologiche e Paleopatologiche, 1993.

Pallottino, Massimo:
Etruscan Painting. Translated by M. E. Stanley and Stuart Gilbert. Cleveland: The World Publishing Co., n.d.
The Etruscans. Edited by David Ridgway, translated by J. Cremona. London: Penguin Books, 1975.
A History of Earliest Italy. Translated by Martin Ryle and Kate Soper. Ann Arbor: The University of Michigan Press, 1991.

Pareti, Luigi. *La Tomba Regolini-Galassi nel Museum Gregoriano Etrusco e la Civiltà dell'Italia Centrale nel VII Sec. aC.* Vatican City: 1947.

Phillips, Kyle M. *In the Hills of Tuscany: Recent Excavations at the Etruscan Site of Poggio Civitate (Murlo, Siena).* Philadelphia: The University Museum, University of Pennsylvania, 1993.

Pittura Etrusca al Museo di Villa Guilia, Studi di Archeologia, 6. Rome: Soprintendenza Archeologica per l'Etruria Meridionale, 1989.

Pomodoro, Arnaldo. *Intimations of Egypt.* San Francisco: Stephen Wirtz Gallery, 1985.

Pope-Hennessy, John. *Cellini.* New York: Abbeville Press, 1985.

Potter, T. W. *The Changing Landscape of South Etruria.* New York: St. Martin's Press, 1979.

Rasmussen, Tom B. *Bucchero Pottery from Southern Etruria.* Cambridge: Cambridge University Press, 1979.

Reed, Henry Hope. *Palladio's Architecture and Its Influence.* New York: Dover Publications, 1980.

Reilly, Robin, and George Savage. *The Dictionary of Wedgwood.* London: Antique Collectors' Club Ltd., 1980.

Rhodes, Dennis E. *Dennis of Etruria: The Life of George Dennis.* London: Cecil & Amelia Woolf, 1973.

Ridgway, David:
The First Western Greeks. London: Cambridge University Press, 1992.
"The Trading Port of Pithekoussai." In *Old World Civilizations: The Rise of Cities and States.* Edited by Göran Burenhult. McMahons Point NSW, Australia: Weldon Owen Pty., 1994.

Ridgway, David, and Francesca R. Ridgway (eds.):
Etruscan Painting. New York: Harcourt Brace Jovanovich, 1986.
Italy before the Romans: The Iron Age, Orientalizing and Etruscan Periods. London: Academic Press, 1979.

Rud, Einar. *Vasari's Life and Lives: The First Art Historian.* Princeton: D. Van Nostrand, 1963.

Rykwert, Joseph, and Anne Rykwert. *Robert and James Adam: The Men and the Style.* New York: Rizzoli, 1985.

Settis, Salvatore (ed.). *The Land of the Etruscans from Prehistory to the Middle Ages.* Florence: Scala, 1985.

Spina. Ferrara, Italy: Comitato Ferrara Arte, 1993.

Spivey, Nigel, and Simon Stoddart. *Etruscan Italy.* London: B.T. Batsford Ltd., 1990.

Sprenger, Maja, and Gilda Bartoloni. *The Etruscans: Their History, Art, and Architecture.* New York: Harry N. Abrams, 1983.

Thorndike, Joseph J. *The Magnificent Builders and Their Dream Houses.* New York: American Heritage, 1978.

Thuillier, Jean-Paul. *Les Étrusques: La Fin d'Un Mystère?* Paris: Gallimard, 1990.

Van Der Meer, L. B. *The Bronze Liver of Piacenza* (Vol. 2). Amsterdam: J.C. Gieben, 1987.

Vickers, Michael. *Ancient Rome.* Oxford: Phaidon Press, 1989.

Wanscher, Ole. *The Art of Furniture: 5000 Years of Furniture and Interi-

ors.* New York: Reinhold Publishing, 1966.

Wellard, James. *The Search for the Etruscans.* New York: Saturday Review Press, 1973.

Wiencek, Henry. *The Smithsonian Guide to Historic America: Virginia and the Capital Region.* New York: Stewart, Tabori & Chang, 1989.

Wilton-Ely, John. *The Mind and Art of Giovanni Battista Piranesi.* London: Thames and Hudson, 1978.

Woodforde, John. *The Strange Story of False Teeth.* New York: Universe Books, 1968.

PERIODICALS:

Barker, Graeme. "Archaeology and the Etruscan Countryside." *Antiquity.* December 1988.

Bonfante (Warren), Larissa. "Etruscan Women: A Question of Interpretation." *Archaeology.* October 1973.

Bonfante, Larissa. "Historical Art: Etruscan and Early Roman." *American Journal of Ancient History,* Vol. 3, 1978.

Bound, Mensun. "Giglio: The Search for the Etruscan Wreck." *Minerva.* January 1990.

Colonna, Giovanni. "The Sanctuary at Pyrgi in Etruria." Translated by Lionel Casson. *Archaeology.* January 1966.

Cristofani, Mauro, and Adriano Maggiani. "La Religione Degli Etruschi." *Archeo.* August 1992.

de Grummond, Nancy. "Thy Name Is Woman." *FMR.* October 1985.

Dingemans, Timothy. "The Search for the Etruscan Wreck of Giglio Island." *Sea History.* Autumn 1993.

Gore, Rick. "The Eternal Etruscans." *National Geographic.* June 1988.

Govi, Cristiana Morigi. *Bologna.* March 1989.

Lerici, Carlo M. "Periscope Camera Pierces Ancient Tombs to Reveal 2,500-year-old Frescoes." *National Geographic.* September 1959.

Nielsen, Erik O. "Some Preliminary Thoughts on New and Old Terracottas." *Opuscula Romana.* May 16, 1987.

Pallottino, Massimo. "New Etruscan Texts on Gold Found at Pyrgi." *Illustrated London News.* February 13, 1965.

Phillips, Kyle Meredith. "Poggio Civi-

tate." *Archaeology.* October 1968.
Pic, Rafael. "Italie: Spina, Une Cité Gréco-Étrusque Engloutie." *Archeologia.* January 1994.
Rasmussen, Tom B. "Archaeology in Etruria, 1980-85." *Archaeological Reports for 1985-86.* British School at Athens, 1986.
Suro, Roberto. "American Students Dig into Etruscan History." *New York Times.* August 5, 1986.

OTHER SOURCES:
Bound, Mensun. "ENAAIA Supplement 1," 1991.
Bound, Mensun. "The Etruscan Wreck." Pamphlet. 1991.
"Case e Palazzi d'Etruria." Catalog. Milan, 1985.
"La Cortona dei Principes." Catalog. Cortona, 1992.
"La Formazione della Città in Emilia-Romagna." Catalog. Bologna, 1987.
Mansuelli, Guido A., et al. "Guida alla Citta' Etrusca e al Museo di Marzabotto." Catalog. Bologna, 1982.
Nielsen, Erik O.:
"Speculations on an Ivory Workshop of the Orientalizing Period." Mediterranean Archaeology Publication. Providence, R.I.: Brown University, 1984.
"Excavations at Poggio Civitate." *Studi e Materiali.* Pamphlet. Giunta Regionale Toscana, 1991.
"Scrivere Etrusco." Catalog. Milan, 1985.
Sorrentino, Giovanna. "Guide to Etruscan Art in Roman Museums." Pamphlet. Rome, n.d.
"Vatican Museums: Egyptians and Etruscans." Florence, 1983.

INDEX

N

BRONZE LIVER

•Marseilles

MEDITERRANEAN SEA

CORSICA

•Florence

•Rome

SICILY

Athens •

•Carthage

SARDINIA